USEFUL T
ON

(Area (

GENERAL INFORMATION

Capitol Switchboard	224-3121

STATUS OF LEGISLATION

Status of bills and scheduled committee hearings on legislation.

Legislative Status Office (LEGIS)	225-1772
Senate Library	224-2971

LEGISLATIVE DOCUMENTS

Copies of bills, resolutions, calendars, committee and conference reports, and public laws may be obtained here.

Senate Document Room	224-7860
House Document Room	225-3456

LEGISLATIVE MEETINGS/FLOOR SCHEDULE

Information on legislative scheduling, meetings, floor proceedings, and congressional recess periods may be obtained here. Recorded information also provides legislative and floor schedules.

Senate Leadership Offices

Majority Leader (Republican)	224-3135
Assistant Majority Leader	224-2708
Minority Leader (Democrat)	224-5556
Minority Whip	224-2158

Recorded Information

Democratic Cloakroom	224-8541
Republican Cloakroom	224-8601

House Leadership Offices

Speaker of the House	225-0600
Majority Leader (Republican)	225-4000
Majority Whip	225-0197
Minority Leader (Democrat)	225-0100
Minority Whip	225-3130

Recorded Information: Floor Proceedings

Democratic Cloakroom	225-7400
Republican Cloakroom.	225-7430

Recorded Information: Legislative Schedule

Democrat	225-1600
Republican	225-2020

Preface

The congressional elections of 1994 brought power to new places on Capitol Hill. For the first time in 40 years, the Republican party holds the majority of the seats in the U.S. House of Representatives. This party also gained control of the U.S. Senate as well but had held this house of Congress in recent years from 1980 to 1986. With the legislative branch of government controlled by the Republican party in the 104th Congress and the executive branch held by the Democrats, divided government has once again returned to Washington. What about the dynamics?

What follows is a general outline of the new people and procedures for the 104th Congress. On both sides of Capitol Hill new leaders direct the Republican and Democratic parties. While the basic legislative process remains the same, procedural changes have occurred for committee and subcommittee action as well as for floor debate, especially in the House.

For nearly 15 years I have been teaching about and observing the operations of the U.S. Congress, the legislative branch of our federal system of government. What has struck me over time is the representative nature of Congress. While most democratically elected legislative bodies in the world ask their lawmakers to make national policy by passing laws, American citizens also ask their congressional politicians, both the representatives and the senators, to represent their interests back home — to keep the military base, build the road, fund the research facility, maintain the campground, or find the lost Social Security check.

Perhaps, the nature of these interests has changed for now. Many of the American people elected politicians to the U.S. Congress in November 1994 who promise to cut taxes, reduce the size of the federal government, and "bring the government home" to the states where it is closer to the people. These reductions seem to be the current interests of many in our country. Republicans who control Congress, and many Democrats as well, have committed to deliver on these requests by the people. I hope that by using my book you will be able to understand procedurally how the members of the 104th Congress will make these changes in government.

Patricia D. Woods, Ph.D.
Executive Director
Woods Institute

Contents

Chapter 1
HOW A BILL BECOMES A LAW   1
   Committee Action, *2*
   Floor Consideration, *5*
   Conference Stage, *6*
   The President's Role, *8*
   The Supreme Court's Role, *8*
   Summary, *8*

Chapter 2
LEADERSHIP AND OTHER POWER CENTERS IN THE U.S. CONGRESS   31
   Leadership on Capitol Hill, *31*
   Organizations on Capitol Hill, *39*
   Summary, *44*

Chapter 3
COMMITTEES ON CAPITOL HILL   45
   Types of Committees, *46*
   Summary, *52*

Chapter 4
COMMITTEES AND THE HEARING PROCESS IN CONGRESS   53
   Membership on a Committee, *53*
   Types of Committee Hearings, *56*
   Summary, *64*

Chapter 5
CONGRESSIONAL STAFF ON CAPITOL HILL 65
   Profile of Congressional Staffers, *66*
   Types of Staff on Capitol Hill, *68*
   Personal Staff in the House and the Senate, *71*
   Committee Staff on Capitol Hill, *73*
   Legislative Support Agencies, *75*
   Summary, *77*

Chapter 6
THE PRESIDENT AS LEGISLATOR 79
   The Chief Executive and Capitol Hill, *79*
   The White House Lobbies on Capitol Hill, *82*
   Executive Agency Liaison with Capitol Hill, *87*
   The President and the National Budget, *88*
   Summary, *90*

Chapter 7
THE FEDERAL BUDGET AND THE CONGRESSIONAL BUDGET PROCESS 91
   The Federal Budget and the Executive Branch, *93*
   Congressional Budget Process, *93*
   The Four Phases of the Budget Process, *97*
   The Realities of the Budget Process on Capitol Hill, *100*
   Summary, *101*

Chapter 8
LOBBYING ON CAPITOL HILL 103

Chapter 9
GETTING AROUND ON CAPITOL HILL 109
   Transportation to Capitol Hill, *109*
   House and Senate Office Buildings, *110*
   Visitors' Access and Security, *112*
   Access for the Physically Disabled, *113*
   Attendance at Congressional Committee Hearings, *116*
   Attendance at the House and Senate

Galleries, *116*
House and Senate Floor Action, *116*

APPENDIXES
A. The Congressional Budget Process Timetable, *121*
B. Committees in the U.S. Congress, *123*
C. Suggested Readings, *141*
D. Woods Institute Service Profile, *143*

GLOSSARY   **145**
INDEX   **149**

Illustrations

The Course of Legislation	3
101st Congress and the Grand Island National Recreation Area Act	10
Legislative Documents	11–29
Leadership on Capitol Hill	33
Party Organizations on Capitol Hill	40
Committees in Congress	48
Hearings on Capitol Hill	57
Legislative Staff and Agencies	67
Information Resources in the Administration and Congress	84
Map of Capitol Hill	111
The House Chamber	119
The Senate Chamber	120

CHAPTER 1

How a Bill Becomes a Law

To understand the legislative process is to understand the nature of the U.S. Congress. It is the only democratically elected national assembly in the world that both represents and legislates. These two hats worn by senators and representatives must be kept in mind when the outside observer of a seemingly chaotic Congress offers the criticism that "nothing ever gets done on Capitol Hill."

One of the reasons that Congress "works" is because it does not work smoothly. Congress was meant to be a deliberative body. This slow process of lawmaking has resulted in a government that has remained free from tyranny for more than 200 years.

Members of the U.S. Congress hold their seats because they are elected by "the people back home" who expect their interests to be represented at the national level. A senator represents an entire state while a House member represents a district of between 550,000 and 800,000 people. Answering to a constituency group every 2 (House) or 6 (Senate) years ensures that members of Congress keep the interests of their states and districts in mind when they put on the lawmaker's hat. In fact, much of the legislation drafted and eventually signed into law closely reflects the needs and interests of the voters throughout the country.

At the beginning of each new Congress — in early January in the odd-numbered calendar years — bills and resolutions are introduced in both the House and the Senate. (The 104th Congress was sworn in on January 4, 1995.) As many as 10,000 pieces of legislation may be submitted for consideration over the next 2 years, the length of each Congress. Proposed laws may relate to issues ranging from pollution to obesity to MX missiles to import duties to violence in professional football.

Congress is a bicameral legislature, and all bills must pass both the House and the Senate before being signed into law by the President. When the bills are dropped into the hopper in each chamber, the "grinding" process for the final product begins (see chart on p. 3).

The parliamentarians of the House and the Senate together with the leadership in each house refer the bill to the designated standing committee that has jurisdiction over the issue. For example, all social security legislation is referred to the Committee on Finance in the Senate and to the Committee on Ways and Means in the House. Each of these committees has a special subcommittee to review all legislation on social security. Falling under a clear jurisdiction of only one committee or subcommittee in each house greatly eases a bill's progress through the legislative process.

Much legislation does not receive such straightforward referral to committee. The leadership may determine that a bill addresses a variety of issue areas; thus, the legislation moves through the slow process of examination by several committees and subcommittees. Other means of referral include split referral and sequential referral (see pp. 49–50 for an explanation of these terms). Joint referral has been eliminated in the House. An example of how legislation can be bogged down because of overlapping committee jurisdiction is the Omnibus Trade and Competitiveness Act of 1988, which was considered by more than 25 committees and subcommittees in the House and Senate.

COMMITTEE ACTION

Just because a bill is introduced and referred to committee does not mean that it will ever move to the hearing stage, since

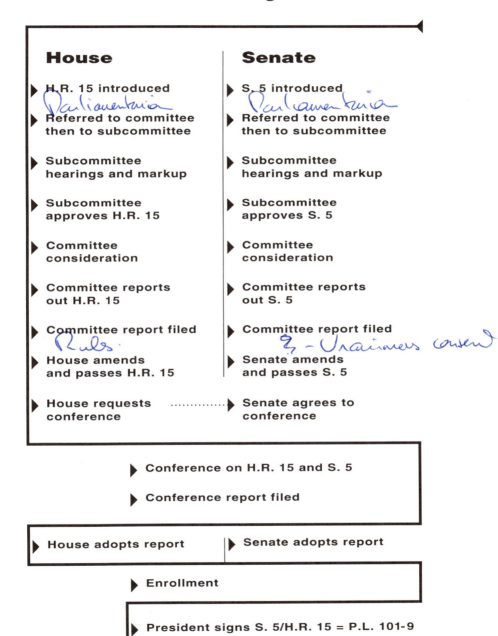

the hearings usually begin at the subcommittee level. Most legislation "dies" in committee from lack of interest.

One of the real challenges on Capitol Hill is to generate interest in an issue and get a hearing scheduled. Holding press conferences, writing letters to other members, obtaining letters from voters, gaining presidential interest, and activating public or private interest groups are all tactics that a representative or senator can use to get a hearing on his or her bill.

Finally, generating the interest of the subcommittee chairperson is another crucial means. If the chairperson decides to conduct a hearing, some of the witnesses from his or her district may be invited to testify. The power of the chairpersons of these committees and subcommittees also is wielded by scheduling, or not scheduling, hearings and by inviting favorable or opposing witnesses to testify.

After all testimony is gathered, the subcommittee, with the help of its staff, begins the "markup." At this point the real crafting of legislation begins, as amendments to change the bill are offered by committee members.

Now is when the work of lobbyists, interest groups, and executive agency personnel who favor or oppose the bill may or may not pay off. Finding a subcommittee member or members to sponsor an amendment to a piece of legislation generally describes a large part of the work of hundreds of people, the lobbyists, who roam the halls on Capitol Hill.

Amendments agreed to in subcommittee are incorporated into the bill which, on final vote, is reported to the full committee. At the full committee level, additional hearings may be held and more amendments may be offered. If, for instance, a lobbying group failed to have an amendment adopted in subcommittee, it can try to find other sponsoring members on the full committee. Again, however, the power and interest of the chairperson can be seen in his ability to schedule hearings on legislation. For example, in the 99th and 100th congresses, the chairperson of the House Committee on Energy and Commerce, John Dingell, opposed the work on the Clean Air Act amendments that the Subcommittee on Health had completed. Many months elapsed before he finally held full committee hearings on the bill.

FLOOR CONSIDERATION

When a bill is approved by the full committee in the Senate, the bill's sponsor works with the leadership to schedule floor consideration. Being a smaller body, the Senate operates very much like a club whose 100 members "unanimously consent" to the proceedings in their chamber. The Senate leadership takes into account the senators' meeting schedules, speaking engagements, and travel plans in an effort to arrange for the Senate's business to be transacted in accordance with the membership's wishes.

Indeed, this informality spills over onto the Senate floor when debate on the proposed law takes place. Unlike the House, amendments, both germane and nongermane, may be offered from the floor by any senator at any time. Debate is unlimited in the Senate but not in the House. "Filibustering" or monopolizing the floor for as many as 74 days, as in the case of the civil rights bill in 1964, may take place in the Senate and not in the House.

A far less casual arrangement exists in the House of Representatives, a legislative body consisting of 435 voting members. Another five members — representing the District of Columbia, Puert Rico, the Virgin Islands, Guam, and American Samoa — can vote in committee but not on the House floor. Ordinarily, when a bill is voted out of committee in the House, it is placed on a legislative schedule called a calendar. Although having successfully been heard and approved by committee, much legislation dies on the calendar. (Remember that about 10,000 pieces of legislation are introduced in each Congress with fewer than 1,000 being signed into law.)

To ensure the consideration of important legislation in the House, the Rules Committee acts as the "traffic cop" over the flow of legislation to the House floor. Sponsors of bills appear before this committee, which is closely allied with the House leadership, to petition for a special rule on when and how their bills will be considered by the full House. It determines how long the debate will be, how many, if any, floor amendments will be considered, and when final passage will occur. The will and power of the speaker of the House to control House business is reflected in this committee.

"The speaker likes surprises only on his birthday and not on the floor of the House," responded one staffer of a former speaker when discussing the role of the Rules Committee. Thus, what the "program" for final passage will be in the House of Representatives is well defined before the legislation moves to the floor for a vote. It would make no sense, nor would there be much order, if House rules permitted 435 people to offer any floor amendment at any time.

CONFERENCE STAGE

When a bill has finally passed by a simple majority in both chambers (sometimes this takes 10 to 12 congresses and more than 20 years, as in the case of the copyright law), the differences between the House and Senate versions of the bill must be resolved in conference committee. The art of compromise in the legislative process is still being exercised at this final, very important stage.

Selection of Conferees

The House speaker and Senate majority leader along with the chairperson and ranking minority member of the committees that heard the bill select the House and Senate members who are to serve as conferees. Generally speaking, these committee leaders choose members on their own committees and subcommittees. Sometimes, however, if someone is a known expert on the subject and is not a member of the committee, he or she will also be selected. Conference committees are often larger. For example, in 1989 the conference committee for the savings and loan bill had 102 members.

Conference Negotiations

In this final stage of the legislative process, lobbyists, the political action committees (PACs), "the people back home," and the White House have one more chance to influence the final language of the bill that the President will sign into law. Sometimes legislation that is strongly supported even by a President dies in conference.

This conference stage may last a few hours, several weeks, or many months. Although the conference chairperson is chosen in an ad hoc fashion, he influences the scheduling and pace of the conference and its bargaining negotiations. The staff also participates in the conference process by drafting amendments, working out agreements, and writing the final conference report.

When the committee, the "final court of appeals," has reached agreement, the conference bill and report must be approved by both the House and the Senate — the bill cannot be amended on the floor. However, rules in the House grant prerogative motions authorizing committee chairpersons to make an objection if they oppose legislative or authorizing language inserted in appropriations bills by the Senate or a conference committee. Authorizing chairpersons can debate for an hour on the House floor any language they oppose.

Rejection of the report by either chamber means that it has failed to pass. Acceptance by both houses through a simple majority vote means that the bill has passed and is ready for the President's signature.

THE PRESIDENT'S ROLE

Under the Constitution, the President, as leader of the executive branch of the U.S. government, may veto any law passed by Congress. However, if a two-thirds favorable vote of the active membership in each house of the Congress occurs, the veto is overridden and the bill then becomes law.

President George Bush vetoed 46 bills that the Democratic-controlled 101st and 102nd Congresses were unable to override. In contrast to Bush, President Bill Clinton vetoed no bills passed by the Democratic-controlled 103rd Congress.

THE SUPREME COURT'S ROLE

The judicial branch — in addition to Congress, the legislative branch, and the executive branch — can also be a player in the legislative process. In the early years of the Republic, the right of judicial review by the Supreme Court of congressionally passed legislation was established by Supreme Court Justice John Marshall in a famous case, *Marbury vs. Madison*. The Constitution does not specifically state that the nation's highest court of law could declare as unconstitutional the laws passed by Congress and signed by the President. The 1803 decision on this case, however, set the precedent for judicial review. The third branch of government, the judiciary, can affect the legislative process by declaring legislation unconstitutional.

An example of how a bill moves through the legislative process is illustrated on p. 10. The documents that were involved in the consideration and passage of the bill, H.R. 1472, are depicted on pp. 11–29.

SUMMARY

In the high-tech world of the 1990s, the process that has been outlined appears to be quite inefficient and impractical. Indeed, if robots instead of people were involved perhaps more work would take place more smoothly on Capitol Hill. However, its sensitivity to the needs of American society makes Congress the truly multidimensional and traditional institution that the founding fathers of this country intended more than 200 years ago.

The speed with which the House Republicans' 1994 campaign manifesto, the Contract with America, passed the House of Representatives in the first 100 days of the 104th Congress in 1995 seemed to challenge the traditionally deliberate nature of the legislative branch of government. But because of the design of the legislative process, the Senate slowed the pace of legislation from the House. Indeed, Senate consideration, often followed by a conference committee, may result in the President's signature or veto. And even after bills become laws, the Supreme Court may declare them unconstitutional. Compromise, comity, and cooperation are at the heart — and in the design — of our system of government with its three separate, but equal branches.

101st Congress and the Grand Island National Recreation Area Act

A bill to establish a recreation area in Michigan, H.R. 1472, was introduced into the House of Representatives early in the 101st Congress. After receiving consideration by two committees, it was passed by the House and sent to the Senate. After Senate committee consideration, H.R. 1472 was passed and signed into law by the President in May 1990.

There was no conference on the legislation.

House

1989

- March 16 ▶ H.R. 1472 introduced
- June 8 ▶ Interior and Insular Affairs Committee reports on H.R. 1472
- July 21 ▶ Agriculture Committee reports on H.R. 1472
- ▶ **Rule and resolution for debates set by House Rules Committee**
- July 31 ▶ H.R. 1472 passes House

Senate

- Sept. 7 ▶ H.R. 1472 received in Senate

1990

- March 5 ▶ Energy and Natural Resources Committee reports on H.R. 1472
- March 20 ▶ H.R. 1472 passes Senate*

President

- May 17 ▶ President signs P.L. 101-292

*There is no Rules Committee in the Senate. A ruling of unanimous consent brings a bill to the floor of the Senate.

A Bill as Introduced

101ST CONGRESS
1ST SESSION
H. R. 1472

To establish the Grand Island National Recreation Area in the State of Michigan, and for other purposes.

IN THE HOUSE OF REPRESENTATIVES

MARCH 16, 1989

Mr. KILDEE (for himself, Mr. LEVIN of Michigan, Mr. WOLPE, Mr. HENRY, Mr. BONIOR, Mr. TRAXLER, Mr. CONYERS, Mr. CARR, Mr. DINGELL, Mr. HERTEL, Mr. VANDER JAGT, Mr. FORD of Michigan, and Mr. SCHUETTE) introduced the following bill; which was referred to the Committee on Interior and Insular Affairs

---

A BILL

To establish the Grand Island National Recreation Area in the State of Michigan, and for other purposes.

1 *Be it enacted by the Senate and House of Representa-*
2 *tives of the United States of America in Congress assembled,*
3 **SECTION 1. ESTABLISHMENT OF GRAND ISLAND NATIONAL**
4 **RECREATION AREA.**
5 In order to preserve and protect for present and future
6 generations the outstandingly remarkable values of Grand
7 Island in Lake Superior, Michigan, and to provide for the
8 conservation, protection, and enhancement of its scenic,
9 recreation, fish and wildlife, vegetation, botanical and histori-

Committee Report

101ST CONGRESS 1st Session	HOUSE OF REPRESENTATIVES	REPT. 101-78 Part 1

ESTABLISHING THE GRAND ISLAND NATIONAL RECREATION AREA IN THE STATE OF MICHIGAN, AND FOR OTHER PURPOSES

JUNE 8, 1989.—Ordered to be printed

Mr. UDALL, from the Committee on Interior and Insular Affairs, submitted the following

REPORT

[To accompany H.R. 1472]

[Including cost estimate of the Congressional Budget Office]

The Committee on Interior and Insular Affairs, to whom was referred the bill (H.R. 1472) to establish the Grand Island National Recreation Area in the State of Michigan, and for other purposes, having considered the same report favorably thereon with an amendment and recommend that the bill as amended do pass.

The amendment is as follows:

Page 1, line 3, strike all after the enacting clause and insert the following in lieu thereof:

SECTION 1. ESTABLISHMENT OF GRAND ISLAND NATIONAL RECREATION AREA.

In order to preserve and protect for present and future generations the outstanding resources and values of Grand Island in Lake Superior, Michigan, and for the purposes of providing for the conservation, protection, and enhancement of its scenery, recreation, fish and wildlife, vegetation, botany and historical and cultural resources, there is hereby established the Grand Island National Recreation Area (hereafter in this Act referred to as the "national recreation area"). These resources and values include, but are not limited to, cliffs, caves, beaches, forested appearance, natural biological diversity, and features of early settlement.

SEC. 2. BOUNDARIES.

The national recreation area shall comprise all of Grand Island in Lake Superior, Michigan, and all associated rocks, pinnacles, and islands and islets within one-quarter mile of the shore of Grand Island. The boundaries of the Hiawatha National Forest are hereby extended to include all of the lands within the national recreation area. All such extended boundaries shall be deemed boundaries in existence as of January 1, 1965, for the purposes of section 7 of the Land and Water Conservation Fund Act of 1965 (16 U.S.C. 4601-9). All federally owned lands within the national recreation area on the date of enactment of this Act are hereby components of the National Forest System and shall be administered by the Secretary of Agriculture as provided in this Act.

29-006

Bill Reported by First Committee

Union Calendar No. 110

101ST CONGRESS
1ST SESSION

H. R. 1472

[Report No. 101-78, Part I]

To establish the Grand Island National Recreation Area in the State of Michigan, and for other purposes.

IN THE HOUSE OF REPRESENTATIVES

MARCH 16, 1989

Mr. KILDEE (for himself, Mr. LEVIN of Michigan, Mr. WOLPE, Mr. HENRY, Mr. BONIOR, Mr. TRAXLER, Mr. CONYERS, Mr. CARR, Mr. DINGELL, Mr. HERTEL, Mr. VANDER JAGT, Mr. FORD of Michigan, and Mr. SCHUETTE) introduced the following bill; which was referred to the Committee on Interior and Insular Affairs

JUNE 8, 1989

Reported with an amendment and referred to the Committee on Agriculture for a period ending not later than July 21, 1989, for consideration of such provisions of the bill and amendment as fall within the jurisdiction of that committee pursuant to clause 1(a), rule X

[Strike out all after the enacting clause and insert the part printed in italic]

House Committee Markup
(Legislative Change)

A BILL

To establish the Grand Island National Recreation Area in the State of Michigan, and for other purposes.

1   Be it enacted by the Senate and House of Representa-
2   tives of the United States of America in Congress assembled,
3   SECTION 1. ESTABLISHMENT OF GRAND ISLAND NATIONAL
4   RECREATION AREA.
5   In order to preserve and protect for present and future
6   generations the outstanding resources and values of Grand
7   Island in Lake Superior, Michigan, and for the purposes of
8   providing for the conservation, protection, and enhancement
9   of its scenery, recreation, fish and wildlife, vegetation, botany
10 and historical and cultural resources, there is hereby estab-
11 lished the Grand Island National Recreation Area (hereafter
12 in this Act referred to as the "national recreation area").
13 These resources and values include, but are not limited to,
14 cliffs, caves, beaches, forested appearance, natural biological
15 diversity, and features of early settlement.
16 SEC. 2. BOUNDARIES.
17   The national recreation area shall comprise all of
18 Grand Island in Lake Superior, Michigan, and all associat-
19 ed rocks, pinnacles, and islands and islets within one-quarter
20 mile of the shore of Grand Island. The boundaries of the
21 Hiawatha National Forest are hereby extended to include all
22 of the lands within the national recreation area. All such

How a Bill Becomes a Law

Committee Report by a Second Committee

101ST CONGRESS 1st Session	HOUSE OF REPRESENTATIVES	REPT. 101-78 Part 2

ESTABLISHING THE GRAND ISLAND NATIONAL RECREATION AREA IN THE STATE OF MICHIGAN, AND FOR OTHER PURPOSES

JULY 21, 1989.—Committed to the Committee of the Whole House on the State of the Union and ordered to be printed

Mr. DE LA GARZA, from the Committee on Agriculture, submitted the following

REPORT

[To accompany H.R. 1472]

[Including Congressional Budget Office cost estimate]

The Committee on Agriculture, to whom was referred the bill (H.R. 1472) to establish the Grand Island National Recreation Area in the State of Michigan, and for other purposes, having considered the same, report favorably thereon with an amendment and recommend that the bill as amended do pass.

The amendment is as follows:
Strike out all after the enacting clause and insert the following:

SECTION 1. ESTABLISHMENT OF GRAND ISLAND NATIONAL RECREATION AREA.

In order to preserve and protect for present and future generations the outstanding resources and values of Grand Island in Lake Superior, Michigan, and for the purposes of providing for the conservation, protection, and enhancement of its scenery, recreation, fish and wildlife, vegetation, botany and historical and cultural resources, there is hereby established the Grand Island National Recreation Area (hereafter in this Act referred to as the "national recreation area"). These resources and values include, but are not limited to, cliffs, caves, beaches, forested appearance, natural biological diversity, and features of early settlement.

SEC. 2. BOUNDARIES.

The national recreation area shall comprise all of the Grand Island in Lake Superior, Michigan, and all associated rocks, pinnacles, and islands and islets within one-quarter mile of the shore of Grand Island. The boundaries of the Hiawatha National Forest are hereby extended to include all of the lands within the national recreation area. All such extended boundaries shall be deemed boundaries in existence as of January 1, 1965, for the purposes of section 7 of the Land and Water Conservation Fund Act of 1965 (16 U.S.C. 460*l*-9). All federally owned lands within the national recreation area on the date of enactment of this Act are hereby components of the

19-648

Bill Reported by a Second Committee

Union Calendar No. 110

101ST CONGRESS
1ST SESSION

H. R. 1472

[Report No. 101–78, Parts I and II]

To establish the Grand Island National Recreation Area in the State of Michigan, and for other purposes.

IN THE HOUSE OF REPRESENTATIVES

MARCH 16, 1989

Mr. KILDEE (for himself, Mr. LEVIN of Michigan, Mr. WOLPE, Mr. HENRY, Mr. BONIOR, Mr. TRAXLER, Mr. CONYERS, Mr. CARR, Mr. DINGELL, Mr. HERTEL, Mr. VANDER JAGT, Mr. FORD of Michigan, and Mr. SCHUETTE) introduced the following bill; which was referred to the Committee on Interior and Insular Affairs

JUNE 8, 1989

Reported with an amendment and referred to the Committee on Agriculture for a period ending not later than July 21, 1989, for consideration of such provisions of the bill and amendment as fall within the jurisdiction of that committee pursuant to clause 1(a), rule X

[Strike out all after the enacting clause and insert the part printed in italic]

JULY 21, 1989

Additional sponsors: Mr. PURSELL and Mr. CROCKETT

JULY 21, 1989

Reported from the Committee on Agriculture with an amendment, committed to the Committee of the Whole House on the State of the Union, and ordered to be printed

[Strike out all after the enacting clause and insert the part printed in boldface roman]

[For text of introduced bill, see copy of bill as introduced on March 16, 1989]

A BILL

To establish the Grand Island National Recreation Area in the State of Michigan, and for other purposes.

1 *Be it enacted by the Senate and House of Representa-*
2 *tives of the United States of America in Congress assembled,*
3 *SECTION 1. ESTABLISHMENT OF GRAND ISLAND NATIONAL*
4 *RECREATION AREA.*
5 *In order to preserve and protect for present and future*
6 *generations the outstanding resources and values of Grand*
7 *Island in Lake Superior, Michigan, and for the purposes of*
8 *providing for the conservation, protection, and enhancement*
9 *of its scenery, recreation, fish and wildlife, vegetation, botany*
10 *and historical and cultural resources, there is hereby estab-*
11 *lished the Grand Island National Recreation Area (hereafter*
12 *in this Act referred to as the "national recreation area").*
13 *These resources and values include, but are not limited to,*
14 *cliffs, caves, beaches, forested appearance, natural biological*
15 *diversity, and features of early settlement.*
16 *SEC. 2. BOUNDARIES.*
17 *The national recreation area shall comprise all of*
18 *Grand Island in Lake Superior, Michigan, and all associat-*
19 *ed rocks, pinnacles, and islands and islets within one-quarter*
20 *mile of the shore of Grand Island. The boundaries of the*
21 *Hiawatha National Forest are hereby extended to include all*
22 *of the lands within the national recreation area. All such*

House Committee Markup
(Legislative Change)

1 SEC. 9. *AUTHORIZATION OF APPROPRIATIONS.*

2   (a) A*CQUISITION OF* L*ANDS*.—*There are hereby au-*
3 *thorized to be appropriated an amount not to exceed*
4 *$5,000,000 for the acquisition of land, interests in land, or*
5 *structures within the national recreation area and on the*
6 *mainland as needed for access and administrative facilities.*

7   (b) O*THER* P*URPOSES*.—*In addition to the amounts*
8 *authorized to be appropriated under subsection (a), there are*
9 *authorized to be appropriated not more than $5,000,000 for*
10 *development to carry out the other purposes of this Act.*

11 SECTION 1. ESTABLISHMENT OF GRAND ISLAND NATIONAL
12   RECREATION AREA.

13   **In order to preserve and protect for present**
14 **and future generations the outstanding resources**
15 **and values of Grand Island in Lake Superior,**
16 **Michigan, and for the purposes of providing for**
17 **the conservation, protection, and enhancement of**
18 **its scenery, recreation, fish and wildlife, vegeta-**
19 **tion, botany and historical and cultural resources,**
20 **there is hereby established the Grand Island Na-**
21 **tional Recreation Area (hereafter in this Act re-**
22 **ferred to as the "national recreation area"). These**
23 **resources and values include, but are not limited**
24 **to, cliffs, caves, beaches, forested appearance, nat-**
25 **ural biological diversity, and features of early set-**
26 **tlement.**

How a Bill Becomes a Law

House Takes Up H.R. 1472

Congressional Record

United States of America

PROCEEDINGS AND DEBATES OF THE 101st CONGRESS, FIRST SESSION

Vol. 135   WASHINGTON, MONDAY, JULY 31, 1989   *No. 105*

House of Representatives

period. The BLM and the Minnesota DNR already know the occupation or landholder status of the vast majority of the parcels to be transferred to the State and have attempted to contact all affected landholders to notify them of their options. As a further safeguard against omission of legitimate claims from consideration prior to the transfer, the bill requires that BLM make aggressive efforts to notify Minnesota residents of the status of the lands, of the intent to transfer those lands to the State, and of the options available to landholders occupying those lands. The Bureau of Land Management plans to advertise in local and regional papers in Minnesota and make other efforts to ensure that landholders are properly notified of the impending transfer and are aware of the options of claimants.

Officials of the Minnesota Department of Natural Resources have assured me they will not accept transfer of any lands whose title remains in dispute, clouded or unclear. Further, BLM is committed to resolving title disputes fairly and equitably before transferring lands to the State. This bill provides both impetus to discover and resolve title disputes and a mechanism to facilitate fair resolution of those disputes.

Despite all of the above safeguards, there remains a remote possibility that a landholder with a legitimate claim, acting in good faith, would somehow be unaware of clouded title to the land he or she occupies or would otherwise be unable to apply for fair resolution of a land title dispute before the land is transferred. Painful past experience has shown that, when dealing with land ownership issues, unanticipated claims may arise. Like any legislation, this bill cannot possibly anticipate all situations which may arise. Both the Bureau of Land Management and the Minnesota Department of Natural Resources have assured me that they will work together to attempt to resolve any legitimate land title claims which may arise after the transfer of lands to the State of Minnesota.

Based on my understanding of the bill as expressed above, and the cooperative attitude and assurances of the VENTO] that the House suspend the rules and pass the bill, H.R. 2783, as amended.

The question was taken; and (two-thirds having voted in favor thereof) the rules were suspended and the bill, as amended, was passed.

A motion to reconsider was laid on the table.

ESTABLISHING THE GRAND ISLAND NATIONAL RECREATION AREA IN THE STATE OF MICHIGAN

Mr. VENTO. Mr. Speaker, I move to suspend the rules and pass the bill (H.R. 1472) to establish the Grand Island National Recreation Area in the State of Michigan, and for other purposes, as amended.

The Clerk read as follows:

H.R. 1472

Be it enacted by the Senate and House of Representatives of the United States of America in Congress assembled,

SECTION 1. ESTABLISHMENT OF GRAND ISLAND NATIONAL RECREATION AREA.

In order to preserve and protect for present and future generations the outstanding resources and values of Grand Island in Lake Superior, Michigan, and for the purposes of providing for the conservation, protection, and enhancement of its scenery, recreation, fish and wildlife, vegetation, botany and historical and cultural resources, there is hereby established the Grand Island National Recreation Area (hereafter in this Act referred to as the "national recreation area"). These resources and values include, but are not limited to, cliffs, caves, beaches, forested appearance, natural biological diversity, and features of early settlement.

SEC. 2. BOUNDARIES.

The national recreation area shall comprise all of the Grand Island in Lake Superior, Michigan, and all associated rocks, pinnacles, and islands and islets within one-quarter mile of the shore of Grand Island. The boundaries of the Hiawatha National Forest are hereby extended to include all of the lands within the national recreation area. All such extended boundaries shall be deemed boundaries in existence as of January 1, 1965, for the purposes of section 7 of the Land and Water Conservation Fund Act of 1965 (16 U.S.C. 460l-9). All federally owned lands within the national recreation area on the date of enactment of this Act are hereby components of the National Forest System and shall be administered by owners of privately owned land and homes within the national recreation area shall be afforded access across National Forest System lands.

(2) Consistent with section 7 of this Act, and the purposes of this Act, the Secretary shall provide for and maintain traditional public access, including vehicular roads for general recreational activities such as camping, hiking, hunting, fishing, and trapping.

(3) The Secretary shall permit the use of snowmobiles on Federal lands in the national recreation area in accordance with the rules and regulations of the National Forest System and consistent with the management plan developed pursuant to section 7 of this Act. Such use shall be regulated to protect the resources of the national recreation area in a way that minimizes the degradation of these resources.

(4) Timber management shall be utilized only as a tool to enhance public recreation, scenic quality, game and nongame wildlife species, and the protection and enhancement of threatened, endangered, or sensitive species. Trees damaged or downed due to fire, insects, disease, or blowdown may be utilized, salvaged, or removed from the recreation area as authorized by the Secretary to further the purposes of the national recreation area.

(5) The Secretary shall, after acquiring fee title to at least 10,000 acres of land on Grand Island, provide reasonable war transportation from the mainland to Grand Island. Transportation may be provided through concession, permit, or other means, and a reasonable charge may be imposed. Transportation shall be subject to reasonable regulation by the Secretary and shall not be required when the Secretary deems it to be unsafe because of factors such as weather and water conditions.

(6) The Secretary shall provide through concession, permit, or other means docking and lodge facilities consistent with the management plan developed pursuant to section 7 of this Act.

(7) The Secretary shall take reasonable actions to provide for public health and safety and for the protection of the national recreation area in the event of fire or infestation of insects or disease.

(8) Under the authority of the Act of March 4, 1915, as amended (16 U.S.C. 497), the Secretary shall issue occupancy and use permits for any privately owned home as of the date of Federal acquisition of the land within the national recreation area on which the home is located. Any such permit shall be issued for an initial period of 20 years and shall be renewed thereafter for successive 20-year periods so long as the permittee is in compliance with the purposes of this Act, the terms of the permit, and other applicable rules and regulations. Any such

Final Passage of the Bill

eration of the bill by the Agriculture Committee's Subcommittee on Forests, Family Farms, and Energy, several amendments to the bill, as reported by the Committee on Interior and Insular Affairs, were considered and adopted.

The first would direct the Forest Supervisor of the Hiawatha National Forest to serve as one of three Forest Service employee members of the advisory commission to the recreation area established by section 8 of the bill. All Forest Service members would serve in a nonvoting capacity.

The second amendment adopted by the subcommittee would require the Secretary of Agriculture to consult with the State of Michigan regarding the designation by the Secretary of zones and time periods within which hunting, fishing, or trapping would be prohibited.

Mr. Speaker, I commend the efforts of the sponsor of H.R. 1472, Mr. KILDEE in bringing this matter to the attention of the House. I also want to thank Chairman VOLKMER and the members of the Forests Subcommittee for their efforts, as well as the cooperation of the Hon. BRUCE VENTO, chairman of the Interior Subcommittee on National Parks and Public Lands for allowing us to bring H.R. 1472 to the floor today.

I urge my colleagues to support passage of H.R. 1472.

Mr. VENTO. Mr. Speaker, I have no further requests for time, and I yield back the balance of my time.

Mr. LAGOMARSINO. Mr. Speaker, I have no further requests for time, and I yield back the balance of my time.

The SPEAKER pro tempore (Mr. MONTGOMERY). The question is on the motion offered by the gentleman from Minnesota [Mr. VENTO] that the House suspend the rules and pass the bill, H.R. 1472, as amended.

The question was taken and (two-thirds having voted in favor thereof), the rules were suspended and the bill, as amended, was passed.

A motion to reconsider was laid on the table.

□ 1340

CIVIL AIRCRAFT COLLISION AVOIDANCE SYSTEM ACT

Mr. ANDERSON. Mr. Speaker, I move to suspend the rules and pass the bill (H.R. 2151) to amend the Federal Aviation Act of 1958 to establish a schedule for the installation in certain civil aircraft of the collision avoidance system known as TCAS-II, and for other purposes, as amended.

The Clerk read as follows:

H.R. 2151

Be it enacted by the Senate and House of Representatives of the United States of America in Congress assembled,

SECTION 1. INSTALLATION AND EVALUATION OF COLLISION AVOIDANCE SYSTEMS.

Section 601(f) of the Federal Aviation Act of 1958 (49 U.S.C. App. 1421(f)) is amended—

(1) by redesignating paragraph (3) as paragraph (6); and

(2) by inserting after paragraph (2) the following new paragraphs:

"(3) OPERATIONAL EVALUATION.—The Administrator shall institute, for a 1-year period beginning not later than December 30, 1990, a program for the operational evaluation of the collision avoidance system known as TCAS-II, in order to collect and assess safety and operational data from the civil aircraft equipped with such system. In conducting the program, the Administrator shall encourage the participation of foreign air carriers which operate civil aircraft equipped with such system.

"(4) EXTENSION OF TIME.—If the Administrator determines that extending the deadline contained in paragraph (2) is necessary—

"(A) to promote a safe and orderly transition to operation of a fleet of civil aircraft described in paragraph (2) which is equipped with the collision avoidance system known as TCAS-II, or

"(B) to promote other safety objectives, the Administrator may extend such deadline for a period not to exceed 2 years; except that the Administrator may further extend such deadline if the Administrator determines that such further extension is necessary to promote aviation safety and notifies, in writing, the Committee on Public Works and Transportation of the House of Representatives and the Committee on Commerce, Science, and Transportation of the Senate of such extension at least 90 days before such extension is to take effect.

"(5) COMPATIBILITY OF WINDSHEAR EQUIPMENT INSTALLATION SCHEDULE.—The Administrator shall consider the feasibility and desirability of amending the schedule for the installation of airborne low-altitude windshear equipment in order to make such schedule compatible with the schedule for the installation of the collision avoidance system known as TCAS-II.".

The SPEAKER pro tempore. Is a second demanded?

Mr. HAMMERSCHMIDT. Mr. Speaker, I demand a second.

The SPEAKER pro tempore. Without objection, a second will be considered as ordered.

The gentleman from California [Mr. ANDERSON] will be recognized for 20 minutes, and the gentleman from Arkansas [Mr. HAMMERSCHMIDT] will be recognized for 20 minutes.

The Chair recognizes the gentleman from California [Mr. ANDERSON].

Mr. ANDERSON. Mr. Speaker, I yield myself such time as I may consume.

Mr. Speaker I rise in support of this legislation. This bill reported by the Committee on Public Works and Transportation makes some necessary changes to legislation enacted at the end of 1987.

The 1987 legislation called for all commercial aircraft to be equipped with the new collision avoidance technology known as TCAS by the end of 1991.

Last fall, the Federal Aviation Administration and the industry began expressing concerns that the final compliance schedule may need adjustment to accommodate a large scale operational evaluation of the equipment and to recognize the shortage of adequate maintenance, engineering, and technical capabilities in the aviation industry. The Congressional Office of Technology Assessment has analyzed these concerns and confirmed their validity. The reported legislation provides for a operational evaluation in the early part of the installation program. This legislation also provides the FAA the authority to adjust the schedule of compliance for safety reasons.

I want to commend Chairman OBERSTAR, and our Committee's Republican leaders Congressman HAMMERSCHMIDT, Congressman CLINGER, and my colleague from California Congressman PACKARD for their leadership and contributions to this bill.

Again, I urge Members to support this bill.

Mr. HAMMERSCHMIDT. Mr. Speaker, I yield myself such time as I may consume.

(Mr. HAMMERSCHMIDT asked and was given permission to revise and extend his remarks.)

Mr. HAMMERSCHMIDT. Mr. Speaker, I rise in support of this bill. The gentleman from California [Mr. PACKARD] is to be commended for the initiative he has displayed on this issue. In addition, Chairman ANDERSON, Subcommittee Chairman OBERSTAR, and Mr. CLINGER, the ranking member of the Aviation Subcommittee, deserve credit for the leadership they have shown in this area. There is no doubt that the installation of collision avoidance equipment on aircraft will enhance aviation safety.

The FAA and the industry have been working on a viable collision avoidance device for a long time, some would say for too long a time. After the midair collision over Cerritos, CA, Congress established deadlines in the law for the certification and installation of the traffic alert and collision avoidance system known as TCAS-II.

However, in our committee's hearing last May on this issue, we learned that the deadlines now in the law for TCAS installation may be impractical or, even worse, could lead to unsafe conditions. So far, TCAS has been tested on only one or two planes at a time. When it comes into more widespread use on many more planes, unforeseen problems could develop. That is why it is important to have a phased implementation, as well as an operational test and evaluation period, for the new TCAS system. The law now on the books does not allow time for this.

This bill would permit the FAA to adopt a phased implementation schedule and to conduct a test of the system as it is being phased in. It would set a target of 1993 for the complete installation of TCAS. The FAA could extend this 1993 date but it would face a heavy burden in doing so.

In my view, this bill will allow for a safe and orderly installation of collision avoidance systems. It will keep the FAA's and the airline's "feet to the fire" to ensure that they install this important safety equipment as soon as possible.

Bill Received in the Senate and Referred to Committee

101ST CONGRESS
1ST SESSION
H. R. 1472

IN THE SENATE OF THE UNITED STATES

SEPTEMBER 7 (legislative day, SEPTEMBER 6), 1989

Received; read twice and referred to the Committee on Energy and Natural Resources

AN ACT *

To establish the Grand Island National Recreation Area in the State of Michigan, and for other purposes.

1 *Be it enacted by the Senate and House of Representa-*
2 *tives of the United States of America in Congress assembled,*
3 **SECTION 1. ESTABLISHMENT OF GRAND ISLAND NATIONAL**
4 **RECREATION AREA.**
5 　　In order to preserve and protect for present and future
6 generations the outstanding resources and values of Grand
7 Island in Lake Superior, Michigan, and for the purposes of
8 providing for the conservation, protection, and enhancement
9 of its scenery, recreation, fish and wildlife, vegetation, botany

---

* *Once a bill has passed one house of Congress it is called an act.*

Committee Report

Calendar No. 469

| 101ST CONGRESS 2d Session | SENATE | REPORT 101–248 |

GRAND ISLAND NATIONAL RECREATION AREA IN THE STATE OF MICHIGAN

MARCH 5 (legislative day, JANUARY 23), 1990.—Ordered to be printed

Mr. JOHNSTON, from the Committee on Energy and Natural Resources, submitted the following

REPORT

[To accompany H.R. 1472]

The Committee on Energy and Natural Resources, to which was referred the Act (H.R. 1472) to establish the Grand Island National Recreation Area in the State of Michigan, and for other purposes, having considered the same, reports favorably thereon with amendments and recommends that the Act, as amended, do pass.

The amendments are as follows:
1. On page 1, line 9, strike ", botany".
2. On page 5, line 6, strike "shall" and insert in lieu thereof, "shall, as a condition of acquisition".
3. On page 7, line 16, strike "The" and insert in lieu thereof, "Subject to the provisions of subsection 3(b)(8) and subsection (b) of this section, the".
4. On page 7, line 21, strike "Act." and insert in lieu thereof, "Act: *Provided*, That the Secretary may not acquire any privately owned lands within the national recreation area other than with the consent of the owner so long as the owner agrees to the restrictions contained in subsection (b)(1) of this section and grants the Secretary a right of first refusal as provided in subsection (b)(2) of this section.".

PURPOSE OF THE MEASURE

The purpose of H.R. 1472 is to authorize and direct the Secretary of Agriculture to purchase lands on Grand Island, Michigan, to establish the Grand Island National Recreation Area, to incorporate such area within the Hiawatha National Forest and to implement several management provisions for the National Recreation Area.

Bill Reported by Committee

Calendar No. 469

101ST CONGRESS
2ND SESSION
H. R. 1472

[Report No. 101-248]

IN THE SENATE OF THE UNITED STATES

SEPTEMBER 7 (legislative day, SEPTEMBER 6), 1989

Received; read twice and referred to the Committee on Energy and Natural Resources

MARCH 5 (legislative day, JANUARY 23), 1990

Reported by Mr. JOHNSTON, with amendments

[Omit the part struck through and insert the part printed in italic]

AN ACT

To establish the Grand Island National Recreation Area in the State of Michigan, and for other purposes.

1   *Be it enacted by the Senate and House of Representa-*
2   *tives of the United States of America in Congress assembled,*
3   SECTION 1. ESTABLISHMENT OF GRAND ISLAND NATIONAL
4   RECREATION AREA.
5   In order to preserve and protect for present and future
6   generations the outstanding resources and values of Grand
7   Island in Lake Superior, Michigan, and for the purposes of
8   providing for the conservation, protection, and enhancement

Senate Committee Markup
(Legislative Change)

1   of its scenery, recreation, fish and wildlife, vetetation, ~~but~~
2   ~~any~~ and historical and cultural resources, there is hereby
3   established the Grand Island National Recreation Area (here-
4   after in this Act referred to as the "national recreation
5   area"). These resources and values include, but are not limit-
6   ed to, cliffs, caves, beaches, forested appearance, natural bio-
7   logical diversity, and features of early settlement.
8   SEC. 2. BOUNDARIES.
9   The national recreation area shall comprise all of the
10 Grand Island in Lake Superior, Michigan, and all associated
11 rocks, pinnacles, and islands and islets within one-quarter
12 mile of the shore of Grand Island. The boundaries of the
13 Hiawatha National Forest are hereby extended to include all
14 of the lands within the national recreation area. All such ex-
15 tended boundaries shall be deemed boundaries in existence as
16 of January 1, 1965, for the purposes of section 7 of the Land
17 and Water Conservation Fund Act of 1965 (16 U.S.C. 460l-
18 9). All federally owned lands within the national recreation
19 area on the date of enactment of this Act are hereby compo-
20 nents of the National Forest System and shall be adminis-
21 tered by the Secretary of Agriculture as provided in this Act.
22 SEC. 3. ADMINISTRATION.
23   (a) ADMINISTRATION.—Subject to valid existing rights,
24 the Secretary of Agriculture (hereafter in this Act referred to
25 as the "Secretary") shall administer the national recreation

Senate Takes Up H.R. 1472

Congressional Record

United States of America

PROCEEDINGS AND DEBATES OF THE 101st CONGRESS, SECOND SESSION

Vol. 136   WASHINGTON, TUESDAY, MARCH 20, 1990   No. 30

Senate

The PRESIDING OFFICER. Without objection, it is so ordered.
The message of the President is as follows:

To the Senate of the United States:
I transmit herewith amendments to the Convention of November 22, 1928, concerning International Expositions, as amended (Treaties and other International Acts Series 6548, 6549, 9948, and Treaty Doc. No. 98-1), with a view to receiving the advice and consent of the Senate to their acceptance. I also transmit, for the information of the Senate, the report of the Secretary of State on the amendments.
The main purposes of these amendments are: To halt the proliferation of world fairs by requiring 5-year intervals between such expositions, beginning in 1995; to establish a single category of "registered" international expositions (world fairs); and to create a new category of "recognized" international expositions.
I strongly support these amendments to the Convention concerning International Expositions, as amended, and recommend that the Senate give prompt consideration to the amendments and advise and consent to their acceptance.

GEORGE BUSH.
THE WHITE HOUSE, March 20, 1990.

MEASURE PLACED ON CALENDAR—S. 2306

Mr. BAUCUS. Mr. President, on behalf of Senators HOLLINGS and THURMOND, I ask unanimous consent that S. 2306, a bill to provide relief for national forests damaged by Hurricane Hugo earlier today be placed directly on the calender.
The PRESIDING OFFICER. Without objection, it is so ordered.

ORDER FOR STAR PRINT—SENATE REPORT 101-251

Mr. BAUCUS. Mr. President, on behalf of Senator BIDEN I ask unanimous consent that the report 101-251 to accompany S. 865 be star printed to reflect the changes which I send to the desk.

The PRESIDING OFFICER. Is there objection to the immediate consideration of the bill?
There being no objection, the Senate proceeded to consider the bill.
The PRESIDING OFFICER. The bill is before the Senate and open to amendment. If there be no amendment to be proposed, the question is on the third reading and passage of the bill.
The bill (H.R. 3311) was ordered to a third reading and was read the third time.
The PRESIDING OFFICER. The bill having been read the third time, the question is, Shall the bill pass?
The bill (H.R. 3311) was passed.
Mr. BAUCUS. Mr. President, I move to reconsider the vote by which the bill passed.
Mr. CHAFEE. I move to lay that motion on the table.
The motion to lay on the table was agreed to.

U. S. NAVAL RESERVE MONTH

Mr. BAUCUS. Mr. President, I ask unanimous consent that the Judiciary Committee be discharged from further consideration of Senate Joint Resolution 266 regarding the designation of March 1990 as "United States Naval Reserve Month," and that the Senate proceed to its immediate consideration.
The PRESIDING OFFICER. Without objection, it is so ordered.
The clerk will report.
The assistant legislative clerk read as follows:

A joint resolution (S.J. Res. 266), regarding the designation of March, 1990, as "United States Naval Reserve Month."

The PRESIDING OFFICER. Is there objection to the immediate consideration of the joint resolution?
There being no objection, the Senate proceeded to consider the joint resolution.
The joint resolution (S.J. Res. 266) was considered, ordered to a third reading, read the third time, and passed.
The preamble was agreed to.
The joint resolution, with its preamble, is as follows:

tributing to fleet support;
Whereas the reservists serve as part-time regular Navy personnel which economically fulfills important military missions and expands the operational abilities of the Navy around the world;
Whereas thousands of employers throughout the United States and the families of reservists have contributed to the support and encouragement needed for a successful Reserve program;
Whereas many Naval reservists have died while serving the Nation; and
Whereas in recognition of great sacrifice of Naval reservists during peace time and during war: Now, therefore, be it
Resolved by the Senate and House of Representatives of the United States of America in Congress assembled, That March 1990, is designated as "United States Naval Reserve Month", and the President of the United States is authorized and requested to issue a proclamation calling upon the people of the Nation to observe the day with appropriate ceremonies and activities in recognition of the 75th anniversary of the United States Naval Reserve.

Mr. BAUCUS. Mr. President, I move to reconsider the vote by which the joint resolution was passed.
Mr. CHAFEE. I move to lay that motion on the table.
The motion to lay on the table was agreed to.

GRAND ISLAND NATIONAL RECREATION AREA

Mr. BAUCUS. Mr. President, I ask unanimous consent that the Senate proceed to the immediate consideration of Calendar No. 469, H.R. 1472, the Grand Island National Recreational Area bill.
The PRESIDING OFFICER. The clerk will report.
The assistant legislative clerk read as follows:

A bill (H.R. 1472) to establish the Grand Island National Recreation Area in the State of Michigan, and for other purposes.

The PRESIDING OFFICER. Is there objection to the present consideration of the bill?
There being no objection, the Senate proceeded to consider the bill.

Final Passage of the Bill

S 2816　　　　　CONGRESSIONAL RECORD — SENATE　　　　　March 20, 1990

AMENDMENT NO. 1346

(Purpose: To make certain technical amendments)

Mr. BAUCUS. Mr. President, on behalf of of Senator RIEGLE, I send four technical amendments to the desk, en bloc, and I ask for their immediate consideration, en bloc.

The PRESIDING OFFICER. The clerk will report.

The assistant legislative clerk read as follows:

The Senator from Montana [Mr. BAUCUS], for Mr. RIEGLE, proposes an amendment numbered 1346.

Mr. BAUCUS. Mr. President, I ask unanimous consent that reading of the amendment be dispensed with.

The PRESIDING OFFICER. Without objection, it is so ordered.

The amendment is as follows:

On page 5, line 23, insert ", stepchildren," after "children".
On page 7, lines 10 and 11, strike "the date of enactment of this Act" and insert "January 1, 1990".
On page 8, line 14, strike "historically consistent" and insert "architecturally compatible".
On page 9, line 11 insert "stepchildren," after "adopted),".

Mr. RIEGLE. Mr. President, I rise today on the occasion of the enactment of H.R. 1472, a bill creating the Grand Island National Recreation Area. The bill will add one of Michigan's greatest wild areas to our national recreation system and open up the opportunity for many Americans to enjoy the island's splendor.

Grand Island is a unique natural treasure of unparalleled beauty. From the pristine and isolated beaches to the imposing shear cliffs rising 200 feet above Lake Superior, this island is a wonder to behold. In the interior of the island you will find the world's third largest beaver-formed lake. Eagles, bear, and numerous other kinds of wildlife make the island their home.

This bill represents three years of careful discussion resulting in a measure acceptable to the parties concerned with this proposed recreation area. The islanders, who now have exclusive access to the island, are ready to share their seasonal home with the Nation. They are willing to do this with the knowledge that their island will be forever protected from unbridled development and unsound environmental practices. The people of Munising have agreed to this plan because they have come to realize that the qualities that make Grand Island a valuable economic resource are beauty, isolation, and quiet grandeur. Through the careful management of the Forest Service, many people will be able to enjoy this unique resource and will, I hope, leave with a new spirit of commitment to preserving our public lands.

The compromise that is represented by H.R. 1472 demonstrates that by working together we can reconcile the need for limited development and protection of fragile and unique resources. While 55 acres of the island are slated for development consistent with the forest management plan, over 12,000 acres will remain undeveloped and timber cuts are forbidden. Some roads will remain open to motorized vehicles, while others will be reserved for hiking only. Under the Forest Service planning process, with strong public involvement, Grand Island will be accessible to all.

I commend the people of Munising, the summer residents of Grand Island, the conservation community and local officials for their patience and willingness to develop a bill that is fair to all parties involved in this project. We must continue to work together to preserve our valuable wild areas places so future generations can experience this important part of our national heritage.

The PRESIDING OFFICER. The question is on agreeing to the amendment.

The amendment (No. 1346) was agreed to.

Mr. BAUCUS. Mr. President, I move to reconsider the vote.

Mr. CHAFEE. I move to lay that motion on the table.

The motion to lay on the table was agreed to.

The PRESIDING OFFICER. If there be no further amendment to be proposed, the question is on agreeing to the committee amendment in the nature of a substitute, as amended.

The committee amendment, as amended, was agreed to.

The PRESIDING OFFICER. The question is on the engrossment of the committee amendment, as amended, and third reading of the bill.

The committee amendment, as amended, was ordered to be engrossed, and the bill to be read a third time.

The bill was read a third time.

The PRESIDING OFFICER. The bill having been read the third time, the question is, Shall the bill pass?

So the bill (H.R. 1472), as amended, was passed.

Mr. BAUCUS. Mr. President, I move to reconsider the vote.

Mr. CHAFEE. I move to lay that motion on the table.

The motion to lay on the table was agreed to.

ORDER FOR STAR PRINT—S. 1862

Mr. BAUCUS. Mr. President, I ask unanimous consent that a star print be made of S. 1862, to reflect the change I now send to the desk.

The PRESIDING OFFICER. Without objection, it is so ordered.

POLICE FORCE OF THE NATIONAL ZOOLOGICAL PARK

Mr. BAUCUS. Mr. President, I ask that the Chair lay before the Senate a message from the House of Representatives on S. 1521.

The PRESIDING OFFICER laid before the Senate the following message from the House of Representatives:

Resolved, That the bill from the Senate (S. 1521) entitled "An Act to amend Public Law 91-34 relating to the police force of the National Zoological Park of the Smithsonian Institution, and for other purposes", do pass with the following amendments:

Strike out all after the enacting clause, and insert:

SECTION 1. INCREASE IN THE MAXIMUM RATES OF BASIC PAY FOR THE POLICE FORCE OF THE NATIONAL ZOOLOGICAL PARK.

(a) IN GENERAL.—Section 5375 of title 5, United States Code, is amended to read as follows:

"§ 5375. Police force of the National Zoological Park

"The Secretary of the Smithsonian Institution shall fix the annual rates of basic pay for positions on the police force of the National Zoological Park as follows:

"(1) Private, not more than the maximum annual rate of basic pay payable for grade GS-7 of the General Schedule.

"(2) Sergeant, not more than the maximum annual rate of basic pay payable for grade GS-8, of the General Schedule.

"(3) Lieutenant, not more than the maximum annual rate of basic pay payable for grade GS-9 of the General Schedule.

"(4) Captain, not more than the maximum annual rate of basic pay payable for grade GS-10 of the General Schedule.".

(b) CLERICAL AMENDMENT.—The item relating to section 5375 in the table of sections for chapter 53 of title 5, United States Code, is amended to read as follows:

"5375. Police force of the National Zoological Park.".

SEC. 2. EFFECTIVE DATE.

The amendments made by section 1 shall apply with respect to pay periods beginning after the date of the enactment of this Act.

The PRESIDING OFFICER. Mr. President, I move that the Senate concur in the House amendments.

The motion was agreed to.

MEASURE REREFERRED—H.R. 1243

Mr. BAUCUS. Mr. President, I ask unanimous consent that the Commerce Committee be discharged from further consideration of H.R. 1243, regarding Metal Casting Competitiveness Research Centers, and that the bill then be rereferred to the Senate Energy and Natural Resources Committee.

The PRESIDING OFFICER. Without objection, it is so ordered.

ORDERS FOR TOMORROW

RECESS UNTIL 9:15 A.M.; REDUCTION OF THE LEADERS' TIME

Mr. BAUCUS. Mr. President, I ask unanimous consent that when the Senate completes its business today, it stand in recess until 9:15 a.m. Wednesday, March 21, 1990, and that the time for the two leaders be reduced to 7½ minutes each.

The PRESIDING OFFICER. Without objection, it is so ordered.

Enrolled Bill
Signed by the President

One Hundred First Congress of the United States of America

AT THE SECOND SESSION

Begun and held at the City of Washington on Tuesday, the twenty-third day of January, one thousand nine hundred and ninety

An Act

To establish the Grand Island National Recreation Area in the State of Michigan, and for other purposes.

Be it enacted by the Senate and House of Representatives of the United States of America in Congress assembled,

SECTION 1. ESTABLISHMENT OF GRAND ISLAND NATIONAL RECREATION AREA.

In order to preserve and protect for present and future generations the outstanding resources and values of Grand Island in Lake Superior, Michigan, and for the purposes of providing for the conservation, protection, and enhancement of its scenery, recreation, fish and wildlife, vegetation and historical and cultural resources, there is hereby established the Grand Island National Recreation Area (hereafter in this Act referred to as the "national recreation area"). These resources and values include, but are not limited to, cliffs, caves, beaches, forested appearance, natural biological diversity, and features of early settlement.

SEC. 2. BOUNDARIES.

The national recreation area shall comprise all of the Grand Island in Lake Superior, Michigan, and all associated rocks, pinnacles, and islands and islets within one-quarter mile of the shore of Grand Island. The boundaries of the Hiawatha National Forest are hereby extended to include all of the lands within the national recreation area. All such extended boundaries shall be deemed boundaries in existence as of January 1, 1965, for the purposes of section 7 of the Land and Water Conservation Fund Act of 1965 (16 U.S.C. 460l-9). All federally owned lands within the national recreation area on the date of enactment of this Act are hereby components of the National Forest System and shall be administered by the Secretary of Agriculture as provided in this Act.

SEC. 3. ADMINISTRATION.

(a) ADMINISTRATION.—Subject to valid existing rights, the Secretary of Agriculture (hereafter in this Act referred to as the "Secretary") shall administer the national recreation area in accordance with the laws, rules, and regulations applicable to the National Forest System in furtherance of the purposes for which the national recreation area was established.

(b) SPECIAL MANAGEMENT REQUIREMENTS.—The national recreation area also shall be administered according to the following special management requirements:

(1) Subject to such terms and conditions as may be prescribed by the Secretary, including the protection of threatened and endangered species and the protection of other natural, cultural, and scenic values, owners of privately owned land and homes within the national recreation area shall be afforded access across National Forest System lands.

H. R. 1472—7

(b) OTHER PURPOSES.—In addition to the amounts authorized to be appropriated under subsection (a), there are authorized to be appropriated not more than $5,000,000 for development to carry out the other purposes of this Act.

[Signature: Thomas S. Foley]
Speaker of the House of Representatives.

[Signature: Jeff Quayle]
~~Vice President of the United States and~~
~~Acting~~ President of the Senate. pro tempore

APPROVED
MAY 1 7 1990

[Signature: George Bush]

The Public Law

PUBLIC LAW 101-292—MAY 17, 1990   104 STAT. 185

Public Law 101-292
101st Congress

An Act

To establish the Grand Island National Recreation Area in the State of Michigan, and for other purposes.

May 17, 1990
[H.R. 1472]

Be it enacted by the Senate and House of Representatives of the United States of America in Congress assembled,

Conservation.
Environmental protection.
Historic preservation.
National parks, monuments, etc.
16 USC 460aaa.

SECTION 1. ESTABLISHMENT OF GRAND ISLAND NATIONAL RECREATION AREA.

In order to preserve and protect for present and future generations the outstanding resources and values of Grand Island in Lake Superior, Michigan, and for the purposes of providing for the conservation, protection, and enhancement of its scenery, recreation, fish and wildlife, vegetation and historical and cultural resources, there is hereby established the Grand Island National Recreation Area (hereafter in this Act referred to as the "national recreation area"). These resources and values include, but are not limited to, cliffs, caves, beaches, forested appearance, natural biological diversity, and features of early settlement.

SEC. 2. BOUNDARIES.

16 USC 460aaa-1.

The national recreation area shall comprise all of the Grand Island in Lake Superior, Michigan, and all associated rocks, pinnacles, and islands and islets within one-quarter mile of the shore of Grand Island. The boundaries of the Hiawatha National Forest are hereby extended to include all of the lands within the national recreation area. All such extended boundaries shall be deemed boundaries in existence as of January 1, 1965, for the purposes of section 7 of the Land and Water Conservation Fund Act of 1965 (16 U.S.C. 4601-9). All federally owned lands within the national recreation area on the date of enactment of this Act are hereby components of the National Forest System and shall be administered by the Secretary of Agriculture as provided in this Act.

National Forest System.

SEC. 3. ADMINISTRATION.

16 USC 460aaa-2.

(a) ADMINISTRATION.—Subject to valid existing rights, the Secretary of Agriculture (hereafter in this Act referred to as the "Secretary") shall administer the national recreation area in accordance with the laws, rules, and regulations applicable to the National Forest System in furtherance of the purposes for which the national recreation area was established.

(b) SPECIAL MANAGEMENT REQUIREMENTS.—The national recreation area also shall be administered according to the following special management requirements:

    (1) Subject to such terms and conditions as may be prescribed by the Secretary, including the protection of threatened and endangered species and the protection of other natural, cultural, and scenic values, owners of privately owned land and homes within the national recreation area shall be afforded access across National Forest System lands.

CHAPTER 2

LEADERSHIP AND OTHER POWER CENTERS IN THE U.S. CONGRESS

Nowhere is the presence of a political party felt more in the U.S. Congress than in its leadership and organization. At the beginning of each Congress, the members of each party in the Senate and the House choose the people who will lead them over the next 2 years, the life of a Congress. Not only do both the majority and minority parties select their leaders, but also the party organizations are involved in committee assignments. So for purposes of "setting up house," the parties' role is important. However, any notion of parliamentary or party government stops here.

Alongside the activities of the political parties is the independence of the members of Congress whose primary loyalties are to their constituents, the voters back home. Although the members appreciate leadership and the party when they receive committee assignments that will aid in their reelection, they cease to tow the party line on legislation that is not supported by their constituents. The party leadership on Capitol Hill, faced with the strong parochial interests of its membership together with the other bases of power on the Hill, has prompted one political scientist to observe, "Congress is organized, but it is not led."

LEADERSHIP ON CAPITOL HILL

The Constitution requires a speaker of the House of Representatives, and a president and a president pro tempore in the Senate. Over the years, other leadership positions have evolved in both these bodies, namely the majority and minority leaders and the majority and minority whips (see chart on p. 33). Chief among the duties of these leaders is to work for party unity in accomplishing their legislative agendas in the face of fierce local loyalties. Along with their leadership responsibilities come the benefits of larger staffs and office space, higher salaries, priority in recognition on the House or Senate floor, and greater media attention. These leaders, especially the speaker of the House and the Senate majority leader, appear frequently on the national news to discuss various congressional activities.

Leaders in the House of Representatives
The Speaker

Although the Constitution does not require the speaker to come from the House membership, every speaker has been an elected member of that body. Second in line for the office of President of the United States, after the vice president, is the speaker of the House of Representatives who often enjoys the most visibility of any leader on Capitol Hill. All 435 House members elect this powerful figure, but this vote is pro forma since choice is strictly along party lines. Prior to the 104th Congress, the Democrats held the position of speaker for 40 years, from 1955 to 1995. With the congressional elections of 1994, however, the voters elected a majority of Republicans to the House of Representatives where Newt Gingrich of Georgia is now speaker. Republican rules changes at the beginning of this Congress have limited the term of speaker to 8 years, or four congresses.

While the real power in the House was held by committee chairpersons for most of the twentieth century, the position of speaker has once again become more influential and dominant in the activities of the House of Representatives. In the mid-1970s, the Democratic speaker became chairperson of the party's Steering and Policy Committee, which assigned Democrats to committees. The speaker also determined which Democratic

Leadership and Other Power Centers

Leadership on Capitol Hill

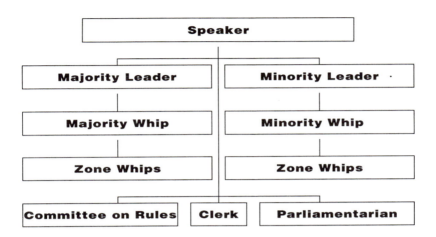

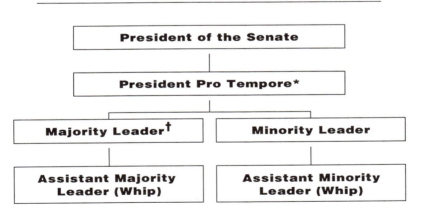

*The president pro tempore merely has presiding authority.
†The majority leader has the power to schedule legislation.

members will be appointed to the House Rules Committee, the "traffic cop" that decides which bills will be considered by the full House. Finally, the speaker, guided by the House parliamentarian, has the power to refer bills to several committees, which can result in the death of legislation. Speaker Gingrich has also controlled committee assignments as well as committee chairmen appointments through the Republican Steering Committee in the 104th Congress.

Democratic speakers of the House of Representatives over the last decade included Thomas "Tip" O'Neill (Massachusetts), Jim Wright (Texas), and Thomas S. Foley (Washington). In contrast to the fragmented nature of the Democratic Party that often has difficulty building a consensus within the party, the Republican Party in the House of Representatives for the 104th Congress is a much more cohesive group, quite willing to follow the leadership of its new speaker to pass the program contained in the House Republicans' campaign manifesto of 1994, the Contract with America. Using Jim Wright's strong style as leader of the House from 1987 to 1989, Speaker Gingrich has garnered much power and is exercising it.

Majority Leader

At the beginning of each Congress, the majority leader is elected by secret ballot of the majority party's conference, the organization to which all members of a party belong. The last five Democratic speakers of the House served as majority leader for the Democrats before being elected speaker, demonstrating why this position is a highly coveted one. It remains to be seen if this position will be a stepping stone to the speakership while the Republicans are in power in the House. The majority leader serves as the party's chief floor leader, promoting party votes, assisting the speaker in the timing and setting of the House legislative agenda, and serving as a liaison with the White House on the President's legislative program, especially if the President is from the same party.

The new majority leader in the House of Representatives is Dick Armey of Texas who has represented his district since 1984. In addition to the responsibilities of this position outlined above, Armey is overseeing personally the passage of the Contract with America through the Republican-controlled House.

Minority Leader

The House minority leader, a Democrat for the first time in 40 years, should have enough parliamentary and legislative experience to lead his colleagues in opposing the legislative measures of the majority party. As titular head of the party, the minority leader encourages party unity for a legislative program both in committee and on the House floor. This is a new position for a Democrat to hold. Party unity has always been difficult for the Democratic Party, which is made up of liberals, moderates, and conservatives, the latter group often voting with the Republicans.

Richard A. Gephardt of Missouri now serves as minority leader. Having been majority leader from 1989 to 1994, he knows the House rules and procedures well. An unsuccessful candidate for the Democratic party's presidential nomination in 1988, Gephardt has a squeaky clean reputation and has been highly regarded by his colleagues for his fairness and his willingness to listen.

The minority leader also chairs the important party organization, the Democratic Steering Committee, which makes the committee assignments for Democratic members, and also serves as an ex officio member of the Democratic Policy Committee, which formulates the party's legislative program.

Majority and Minority Whips

Serving as an assistant to the majority or minority leader, the whip constantly works for party discipline and unity behind a legislative program. Assisted by regional whips or zone whips, the whip's organizations make head counts for final votes, gather information for the leadership regarding the party's overall attitude on an issue, and work to persuade or "whip" the party's membership in line. The new Republican whip is Tom DeLay of Texas. The minority whip is Democrat David Bonior of Michigan.

The whip organizations are so very much a part of the leadership structure that they are responsible for tracking weekly floor activity. The "whip notice," published by the majority party late on Thursday of each week while the House is in session, contains a list of the legislation to be considered for final passage on the House floor the following week.

The Republican whip is chosen by the Republican Conference, which is composed of all Republican members of the House of Representatives. The Democratic representatives elect the whip in the Democratic Caucus, the Democratic party organization, at the beginning of each Congress.

Leaders in the Senate
President of the Senate

The Constitution provides that the vice president of the United States serve as the president of the Senate. Presiding rarely over this chamber, the vice president does have the power to cast tie-breaking votes, the only vote that he can make in the Senate. With the separation of powers in U.S. government, the position of president of the Senate is the only official participatory role the executive branch has on Capitol Hill.

President Pro Tempore

A second Senate officer, the president pro tempore, is called for in the Constitution to preside over the Senate in the absence of the Senate president. This office is third in line, after the vice president and the speaker of the House, to assume the presidency in an emergency.

Tradition holds that the position of president pro tempore is reserved for the member of the majority party who has served in the Senate for the longest, most continuous period of time. In the 104th Congress, Strom Thurmond of South Carolina holds this position. Neither the Senate president nor the president pro tempore has the power and influence as presiding officer that the speaker of the House of Representatives enjoys.

Majority Leader

As the party's floor leader, the majority leader is chief strategist for passage of the party's legislative program. The personalized, informal nature of the "Club of 100" (the U.S. Senate) defines this position as one of persuasion, compromise, and conciliation. Elected at the beginning of each Congress, this Senate leader is responsible for scheduling bills on the floor and serving as liaison with the White House if the President is from the same party. Rules for floor consideration of bills are fewer and less strict than those in the House. Therefore, none of the presiding officers nor the majority leader has the power the speaker of the House has to control debate. Unlike the House Rules Committee, the Senate Rules Committee oversees Senate administrative issues such as office space rather than regulations on amendments and legislation for floor consideration.

Style and personality contribute to a majority leader's success. In recent years, leaders such as Howard Baker, a Republican from Tennessee, had the talents and personal touch so necessary to hold together the factions within the Republican party in the early 1980s. Such leadership ability enabled the White House to achieve budget and tax cuts, the Reagan Revolution, in the summer of 1981.

When the Republicans gained control of the Senate for the 104th Congress, they elected Robert Dole of Kansas to be their majority leader. Dole served as majority leader in the 99th Congress, when the Republicans controlled the Senate. First elected to this body in 1968, Sen. Dole ran for the vice presidency with Gerald Ford in 1976. From 1980 to 1984, during the 97th and 98th congresses, he served as chairperson of the Senate Finance Committee. His leadership during tight budget times has been especially strong. As minority leader during the 103rd Congress at the beginning of Bill Clinton's presidency, Dole, as the leading Republican in Washington, has proved to be a powerful figure. His knowledge of and strategic use of Senate rules and the filibuster were effective tools for obstructing Clinton's legislative agenda and that of the Democrats in the Senate.

Minority Leader

The leader of the minority party in the Senate works for party unity to check and to challenge the activities of the majority party. In the event that the President is a member of the same party as the minority leader, the minority leader guides the chief executive's legislative program through the Senate.

The Democratic senators elected Thomas Daschle of South Dakota to serve as their minority leader during the 104th Congress. A moderate politician from America's heartland, Daschle must work to keep the factions of his party together. Even though the Democrats have only 46 senators in the 104th Congress, unlike the House where the majority in numbers truly rules, the Senate's rules and procedures may permit the minority to prevail as in the case of the defeat by the Republicans of Bill Clinton's economic stimulus package in the spring of 1993 or the failure of the Republican-controlled Senate to pass a proposed balanced budget amendment to the Constitution in the early months of 1995.

Party Whips

The positions and duties of whip in the Senate, whether majority or minority, are similar to those of the whip in the House of Representatives. Working for party unity and counting and predicting votes on legislation, the majority and minority whips assist their leaders in scheduling legislation for floor consideration and lobbying party colleagues. The current whip positions for the 104th Congress in the Senate are held by Republican Trent Lott of Mississippi, the majority whip, and Wendell Ford of Kentucky, the Democratic whip.

ORGANIZATIONS ON CAPITOL HILL

Having described the leadership positions in both houses of Congress, the organizational side of Capitol Hill deserves attention. The political party organizations of committees and conferences, standing legislative committees, and single-issue congressional service organizations comprise the various strata of organizational entities that exist in Congress. Although the leadership endeavors to maintain its control over the legislative activities of its membership, other leaders emerge from each of these strata, a reality that suggests just how dispersed power is on Capitol Hill.

Party Organizations on Capitol Hill

In the House of Representatives, every Republican is a member of the Republican Conference and every Democrat belongs to the Democratic Caucus. The equivalent organizations in the Senate are called the Republican and Democratic conferences. These groups elect the party leaders, approve committee assignments, discuss party legislative strategies and policy, and sometimes discipline party members by stripping them of their committee assignments.

An example of a party disciplining one of its members is the case of Rep. Phil Gramm, a Democrat from Texas. As a member

Party Organizations on Capitol Hill

House

Republican Conference
- Steering Committee
- Policy Committee
- Campaign Committee

Democratic Caucus
- Steering Committee
- Policy Committee
- Campaign Committee

Senate

Republican Conference
- Committee on Committees
- Campaign Committee
- Policy Committee

Democratic Conference
- Steering Committee
- Campaign Committee
- Policy Committee

of the House Budget Committee in 1981, Gramm was privy to the Democrats' plans for opposing the President's budget, plans which he revealed to the Republicans. The Democrats lost all major votes on the budget that summer. On its leadership's recommendation in 1983, the Democratic Party refused to give Gramm his seat on the Budget Committee for the 98th Congress. Very rarely does such reprimanding take place on Capitol Hill. After this party disciplinary action, however, Phil Gramm resigned his seat, switched to the Republican party in 1983, and was reelected to the same seat to serve as a Republican on the Budget Committee. In 1984, he was elected a U.S. senator from Texas.

At the beginning of the 100th Congress, the Democratic Caucus again wielded its power when it initially denied Les Aspin the role of chairperson of the House Armed Services Committee. Many members felt that Aspin had betrayed them in the 99th Congress when, as chairperson of this important committee, he had voted for the MX missile as well as aid to the contras. Ultimately, Aspin regained his position as chairperson after several weeks of intense lobbying of his colleagues.

There are another dozen or so party groups in the House and the Senate. The functions and names of the most important ones follow.

House Republicans

The Republican Steering Committee consists of 26 members who determine all committee assignments. Of this number, three are members of the freshman class elected to Congress in 1994.

The Republican Policy Committee consists of 41 people who work to unite the party and to set a party policy and strategy. Seven of these people were elected to Congress in 1994.

The National Republican Congressional Committee assists

in the campaigns of new candidates for the House and also aids Republican members in their reelection campaigns.

Currently, under Republican party rules in the House, no committee chairperson may hold his or her position for more than three congresses or 6 years.

House Democrats

The Democratic Steering Committee has 29 members, including the Democratic Leader. It makes committee assignments for the Democrats and works closely with the party's caucus. The Democratic Leader appoints nine members, which include four chief deputy whips, to the steering committee. Another 12 members are elected by House representatives from the 12 geographical regions of the country. The remaining eight members are Democratic party leaders and senior committee ranking members from panels such as Appropriations, Ways and Means, and Rules.

The Democratic Policy Committee consists of up to 36 members, with the Democratic Leader serving as the chairperson. The function of the Policy Committee is to assist the Democratic Caucus in establishing the party's policy agenda and legislative priorities.

The Democratic Congressional Campaign Committee helps in the election and reelection of Democrats to the House.

Senate Republicans

The Republican Committee on Committees makes all of the committee assignments of Republican senators.

The Republican Policy Committee helps research, coordinate, and unify the party's policy behind a legislative agenda.

The National Republican Senatorial Committee helps in the election campaign support for Republican candidates for the Senate.

Senate Democrats

There are 25 members of the Democratic Steering Committee in the Senate who make committee assignments that are then offered up to the full Democratic Conference for confirmation.

The 21 members of the Senate Democratic Policy Committee recommend positions for the party to take on proposed legislation. They also work with party leadership to schedule legislation for debate and final consideration on the Senate floor.

The Democratic Senatorial Campaign Committee offers assistance to Democratic candidates for the Senate.

Committee Organizations

Most of the substantive work of drafting legislation takes place in committee on Capitol Hill. Because of this, the role and power of committee and subcommittee chairpersons of the more than 200 committees on the Hill have grown in recent years. In fact, "government by subcommittee" has described the power source scheme in Congress since the late 1970s. If a subcommittee chairperson refuses to hold a hearing on a piece of legislation, there is little, if anything, the party leadership can do. Although viewed by many as a subversion of the power of the leadership and the more senior committee chairpersons, the scattering of power represents, perhaps, a Congress that is more open to and more influenced by outside forces, whether they be constituents, lobbyists, or political action committees.

With the Republicans in charge of the House of Representatives for the first time in 40 years, there have been rules changes in an effort to limit the power of the committee and subcommittee chairmen. The term of a chairperson is limited to six years or three congresses. In addition to this, legislation that is referred to a full committee does not necessarily have to be referred to subcommittee for consideration.

Congressional Member Organizations

Congressional member organizations (CMOs) have replaced issue caucuses in the 104th Congress. A CMO is an informal organization of members of the House of Representatives who join together to share official resources in pursuit of common legislative and research objectives. Funding for such organizations derives from a member's Clerk Hire staff account and other resources under the member's control. These organizations have no separate office space on Capitol Hill and may not use the frank or a member's frank (mailing) privilege. Issue caucuses still exist in the Senate, but the most active and vociferous were at work in the House.

Some of the CMOs that have been formed in the 104th Congress in the House of Representatives include the New York State Delegation, Sunbelt Caucus, and Black Caucus.

SUMMARY

One of the difficulties of understanding Congress for an outsider looking in is the dispersal of power and absence of party authority on Capitol Hill. Unlike the other democratically elected legislative bodies that are also parliamentary forms of government, the Congress of the United States is a representative legislature — a legislature that responds to the interests of voters and not primarily those of party ideology.

CHAPTER 3
Committees on Capitol Hill

Most of the major work of lawmaking in the U.S. Congress takes place in the committees and subcommittees of the U.S. Senate and the House of Representatives. More than 100 years ago Woodrow Wilson wrote, "It is not far from the truth to say that Congress in session is Congress on public exhibition, whilst Congress in its committee rooms is Congress at work." To appreciate better the workings of Capitol Hill, an understanding of the committee system is vital.

With nearly 10,000 pieces of legislation introduced in each Congress, a filtering mechanism must exist to produce the best possible laws. The committees in the House and the Senate provide the needed review function that ultimately results in fewer than 1,000 bills being signed into law every 2 years. These "work groups" draft and craft legislation. The committee process is central to the deliberative path of legislation through both the House and the Senate.

Until the early 1970s, the power of the committees rested with the chairpersons, many of whom had served for more than 20 years in the Senate and 30 years in the House of Representatives. The Democratic majority in the House and the Senate in the 1950s and 1960s meant that its party members could serve as chairpersons of the committees. This "seniority system," as it was called then, closed off the opportunity for younger members of Congress to advance to positions of importance in committee. Before 1973, most committees did not have subcommittees, which suggests that the power of a committee rested totally with the chairperson. Men such as Tom Connelly and Clarence Cannon in the Senate and Wilbur Mills and Wright Patman in the House ruled their committees with an iron hand for many years.

When the younger generation, the so-called "Watergate babies," entered Congress in the early 1970s, they demanded greater participation in the committee system. Through rules changes in the House and the Senate, they succeeded in establishing a more open committee system in terms of membership and work activity. This "victory" by the younger members led to a growth in the number of subcommittees from 1975 to 1995, making the legislative process all the more complex and confusing to the outsider. With more than 250 committees and subcommittees holding hearings on Capitol Hill, the task of following a piece of legislation became a challenge, although not an impossible one.

When the Republicans won control of the House after the elections of 1994, many of their rules changes included a reduction in the number of committees and subcommittees. In an attempt to cut down on jurisdictional overlap and to save money, the House abolished three full committees and 20 subcommittees at the beginning of the 104th Congress in 1995.

TYPES OF COMMITTEES

While the lawmaking committees, referred to as the standing committees, are the most active groups, there are also joint committees, select committees, and conference committees.

Standing Committees

In an effort to implement reforms in Congress, the Republican-controlled House abolished three standing committees at the beginning of the 104th Congress in 1995. These committees include that of the District of Columbia, Merchant Marine and Fisheries, and the Post Office and Civil Service. The Republicans in the House have also renamed many of the full committees along with their subcommittees. For example, the House

Armed Services Committee is now the Committee on National Security, the Committee on Energy and Commerce is now the Commerce Committee, and the former Committee on Natural Resources is now the Committee on Resources.

There are currently 35 standing committees in the Congress — 16 in the Senate and 19 in the House. Covering a broad range of issue areas that touch all aspects of American life, from agriculture to taxes to highways to health care to MX missiles to international trade, these committees draft and amend the legislation referred to them by the parliamentarians in each house.

Each of these committees has several subcommittees. The appropriations committees, the money committees in each body, have the largest number of subcommittees (13). In addition to House Appropriations, the Committee on Government Reform and Oversight has seven subcommittees and that of Transportation and Infrastructure has six subcommittees. New House rules limit the number of subcommittees to five for all other committees. The Senate sets no limits on the number of subcommittees. There may be as few as four or as many as eight subcommittees.

Two categories of standing committees exist in both the House and the Senate. The *authorizing committees* are the programmatic committees and subcommittees that draft laws to create federally funded programs, such as student loans, Medicare, and nuclear aircraft carriers. However, just because a program has been created does not mean that the money will be available for the execution of it. The power to fund programs rests in the *appropriations committees* in the House and the Senate.

As mentioned above, each of these appropriations committees has 13 subcommittees whose powerful chairpersons and membership determine how many dollars will be spent for each program. For example, the Senate Committee on Agriculture may authorize $25 billion for the Food Stamp Program while the Agriculture Subcommittee on Appropriations may have planned

Committees in Congress

Standing Committees

Permanent legislative committees

Authorization

Committees that draft laws to create programs

Appropriations

Committees that fund programs

Study Committees

Nonpermanent special issue committees

Select

Committees that may be formed in each chamber to study special issues

Joint

Combined House and Senate special issue committees

Conference Committees

Ad hoc committees of House and Senate members formed to reach consensus on legislative language in a bill that requires final agreement by both the full House and Senate

for only $20 billion, or perhaps decided not to fund any program at all. To complete a possible scenario, the House of Representatives may have appropriated $18 billion. Since the legislative language must be the same in both houses for a law to be enacted, the differences must be resolved in a final conference.

While money bills receive consideration by committees each year, most legislation sent to committee dies there, never having received a hearing.

If a bill receives any consideration at all, the subcommittee of a full committee with specific jurisdiction normally holds the first hearing. For example, if a bill on a program to build F-18 fighter planes is introduced in the House of Representatives, it is sent to the National Security Committee whose chairperson then refers it to the Subcommittee on Military Acquisition where hearings may take place. In the "mark-up" process, changes may be made to a bill. When these changes are incorporated into the bill, a "clean" bill is then sent to the full committee for consideration.

Although a bill may receive a favorable vote in subcommittee, it still may not be considered by the full committee. If a chairperson does not favor a piece of legislation, he or she can refuse to hold hearings on a bill for many months or not at all. Throughout the 1980s, John Dingell, chairperson of the House Energy and Commerce Committee, delayed hearings or refused to hold hearings on clean air legislation, thus killing the measure in committee. It should be noted here that under new rules in the House, legislation referred to a committee does not have to be referred by the chairperson to a subcommittee for consideration.

The progress of a legislative proposal outlined above occurs if a bill is tightly drafted, that is to say it covers only one issue area. If a bill is broadly drafted, it may receive multiple, split, or sequential referral to committee. Joint referral means that the bill is sent to several committees for consideration. Sequential referral means that the bill must be considered first by one committee and then, following that consideration, by other committees. Split referral means that parts of the bill are to be considered by various committees. For the 104th Congress, through rules changes, joint referral has been abolished in the Republican-controlled House of Representatives.

Let us take the case of split referral for purposes of discussion. If one part of a bill with four parts or titles involves taxes, Senate rules would require that the Ways and Means Committee in the House and the Finance Committee in the Senate consider the section on revenues. It is possible that the other three parts of the bill may be referred to three other committees such as Banking, Commerce, and Public Works. This one means of referral illustrates how much longer it would take for a bill to be considered in full if it covers a broad range of issue areas.

Select Committees

Select or special committees in both the Senate and the House study issues affecting a very specific area. Several of these committees, such as the Senate Select Committee on Aging and the Permanent Select Committee on Intelligence, have become more permanent in nature. Technically established for 2 years, they offer recommendations for legislation.

The hearings of these committees provide forums where the elderly (Senate Select Committees on Aging) and Native Americans (the Senate Select Committee on Indian Affairs) may appear before a committee to make a public statement on the status and problems of the constituents for whom they speak. Often legislation is introduced because of the recommendations that are made by these committees.

In an effort to streamline the work of Congress, the House changed its rules in the 104th Congress to limit its members' service to two on standing committees and to four on subcommittees. There is no such rule in the Senate. While the House abolished its special committees and three standing committees — District of Columbia, Merchant Marine and Fisheries, and Post Office and Civil Service — to save money, the Senate's select committees on Ethics, Indian Affairs, and Intelligence and its Special Committee on Aging continue to exist to make recommendations for legislation.

Joint Committees

Joint committees, consisting of an equal number of senators and representatives, hold hearings that result in policy recommendations in the areas of economics and tax. Generally speaking, the Library of Congress, Printing, Taxation, and Economics joint committees do not draft laws but rather provide in-depth studies for the direction of future legislation. In an effort to save money, some or all of these committees may be abolished in the future.

Conference Committees

A final type of committee on Capitol Hill is the conference committee, or "final board of review" of legislation before it is passed. This committee is formed when a piece of legislation, whether a bill or a joint or concurrent resolution, has passed both the Senate and the House but with different language. Since legislation must pass both the House and the Senate in identical form, differences between the House and Senate versions are resolved "in conference." Until 1975, these conference sessions were closed to the public. However, rules changes in both the Senate and the House opened these meetings to the public. It should be noted that even though the sessions are technically open at the conference stage, the rooms for the conference sessions are often quite small and seating is limited.

The size and membership of this committee, under the rules,

are determined by the leadership of both houses. But in practice, the chairperson and the ranking minority member of a committee involved appoint the representatives and the senators. (In 1988, the conference committee on the omnibus trade bill consisted of 100 conferees.) When a final vote is taken by the conference committee, the committee dissolves.

It should be noted that these groups are quite important to the legislative process. If either the House or the Senate rejects the report of a conference on a piece of legislation, the bill or resolution will fail to clear the remaining legislative hurdles.

SUMMARY

The committee system, so crucial to the lawmaking process on Capitol Hill, reflects the deliberative nature of Congress. With deliberation often comes tension, which can slow the progress of a bill through the legislative channels. Such seemingly excessive examination appears to be uncalled for as well as inefficient. However, another way of looking at this "poor way of doing business" is to realize that Congress, the representative body that it is, reflects the complexities of twentieth-century American society whose fabric is woven so tightly that issue areas of public policy are often closely related to one another.

CHAPTER 4

COMMITTEES AND THE HEARING PROCESS IN CONGRESS

No greater example of the dual roles of representative and lawmaker is there than the activities of senators and representatives in committee. Most of the drafting of legislation takes place in committee. Very closely tied to this lawmaking responsibility are the realities of being an elected representative that often affect the makeup and workload of a committee as well as the nature of the hearings themselves.

MEMBERSHIP ON A COMMITTEE

In November of each election year, all 440 seats in the House and one-third of the Senate seats are open. In the House, newly elected members will be assigned to their first committees and returning members can seek reassignment on the same or other committees. Although fewer changes should occur in the Senate since fewer seats are open for election, committee assignment or reassignment can be a major task among the "Club of 100." Throughout the 1980s, there were more changes than usual as the Senate changed from a Democratic to a Republican majority in 1980, and as the Democrats regained control in 1986.

With the congressional elections of 1994, all committee and subcommittee chairmen in both the House and the Senate changed because the Republicans, with majorities in both chambers, took control of the legislative branch of government. As previously mentioned, new rules in the House have limited the tenure of all chairmen of full committees and subcommittees to three congresses, or 6 years. Also, membership on House committees is limited to no more than two full committees and four subcommittees. The Senate does not have such term limits on committee chairs or on committee assignments.

The leadership organization of each party in the Senate and the House determines committee assignments. The party with the majority of seats in each chamber will assign the committee chairpersons and the ratio of majority to minority committee membership.

When the election is over, another kind of campaign begins, that of the members of Congress to gain seats on the committees of their choice. With an eye toward reelection, especially in the House, members seek assignments to committees with issue areas having the greatest effect on their district or state. Although the committee is the forum for lawmaking, the representative nature of the Congress comes through when the composition of the committees' membership is examined. Generally, the older members who know one another and the leadership fare better in desired committee assignments than the freshmen. However, effective lobbying of the leadership and party colleagues between the election and the new Congress in January can pay off even for new members. It is possible for a new congressman to be on a powerful money committee if he or she has the support of senior members.

The large number of new House members — 86 — in the 104th Congress — 73 of whom are Republicans — meant plum assignments for many newcomers. In an effort to reward many of the newcomers, Speaker Newt Gingrich gave seats to some freshmen on the powerful committees of Appropriations, Ways and Means, and Commerce. Among those Republicans receiving coveted assignments were George Nethercutt (Wash.), Jon Christensen (Neb.), and Mel Reynolds (Ill.), who won places on Appropriations and Ways and Means committees, respectively.

Many new members also kept their constituents' needs in

mind. Republican Tom Latham of Iowa requested and was assigned to the Agriculture Committee in the same way that Democrat Sheila Jackson-Lee of Texas found a place on the Science Committee.

Even the more senior members of Congress keep the people back home in mind. Rep. Floyd Spence, who has represented South Carolina's second district for 24 years, chairs the Committee on National Security, formerly the House Armed Services Committee. Having served on this committee for most of is time in Congress, he appreciates and protects the Navy's presence in South Carolina.

Senate leadership also considers a state's interests when committee assignments are made. Many seats on the Energy and Natural Resources Committee are held by senators from the West, where most of the public lands are located. The appointments of Sen. Larry Craig, a Republican from Idaho, and Sen. Jeff Bingaman, a Democrat from New Mexico, are good examples.

This desire to represent a state or district's interests should not be interpreted as totally undermining the policymaking process of Congress. In fact some committee chairpersons have come from areas of the country that are not directly affected by the issues that they spend hours, days, and even years deliberating. Rep. Lee Hamilton, a Democrat from Indiana, is an individual who — having a safe seat — has worked in areas more international in nature for several years. He is now the ranking minority member of the House International Relations Committee.

Some recent committee assignments in the Senate reflect national issues that concern all of American society. In the 1992 elections, a record number of women — five — was elected to the Senate for the 103rd Congress, bringing the total number to six female senators, one Republican and five Democrats. Many of these women campaigned on platforms for women's issues, especially in the wake of Anita Hill's testimony at the confirmation hearings of Clarence Thomas, a nominee for the Supreme Court set forth by then President George Bush. As a result, Diane Feinstein of California and Carol Moseley-Braun of Illinois have been appointed by the majority leader to serve on the formerly all-white male panel, the Senate Judiciary Committee.

Indeed, a seat on a powerful, prestigious committee in Congress could mean greater influence and media attention to a representative and especially to a senator. Over the years, the stature of committees has changed according to America's interests, international involvement, and needs.

In recent years on Capitol Hill, the tax, budget, and money committees as well as the energy and armed services committees have been among the more powerful and prestigious. During the early 1970s, the Senate Foreign Relations and House Foreign Affairs committees and judiciary committees held national prominence because of Vietnam and Watergate, and membership on these committees was coveted. Today, with the Judiciary Committee in both the Senate and the House having to consider and to vote on the social agenda issues of busing, school prayer, and abortion, few people willingly want to serve as members. On the other hand, the House Committee on Commerce and the Senate Committee on Energy and Natural Resources have become powerful and prestigious committees on which to hold seats. The oil crisis of the 1970s and President Carter's effort to draft an energy legislation package, concern about government deregulation in the 1980s, and the growing environmental movement have contributed to the greater prominence of these committees today.

TYPES OF COMMITTEE HEARINGS

Four types of committee hearings take place in Congress. *Legislative*, *oversight*, and *investigation* hearings are held in both the Senate and the House while the Constitution calls for *confir-*

Hearings on Capitol Hill

Legislative Hearings
▶ Review of specific bills

Oversight Hearings
▶ Ongoing review of established programs

Investigation Hearings
▶ Pursuit of suspected illegal activities

Confirmation Hearings
▶ Senate review of high-level presidential appointees

mation hearings to occur only in the Senate. The location, tone, and timing of these congressional hearings do not evolve in a vacuum. Much of the tone and content of hearings on Capitol Hill have to do with the agenda of a committee's chairperson and his committee staff who are responding to the country's legislative needs, the interests of the people back home, and the lobbying groups in Washington.

Many people complain that hearings are totally orchestrated and often exist merely to provide photo opportunities for members on the nightly news. To a certain extent this is true since the chairperson and committee staff schedule the time and place of the hearings. Depending on the issue, these public hearings (i.e., legislative, oversight, and investigative) may even be held in a representative's home district or senator's state as well as on Capitol Hill. (Hearings that take place outside of Washington are referred to as field hearings.)

Legislative Hearings

The most common hearings are those that consider bills to change existing law. Creation of new federal programs and amendments to or elimination of existing ones take place in legislative hearings. Because of the importance of these lawmaking committees, the discussion of their proceedings will be more involved than that for the oversight, investigative, and confirmation hearings.

Not every bill that is introduced receives a hearing. In fact, most do not and die in committee. Generating interest in a bill presents one of the greatest challenges to a bill's sponsor, especially if the legislation is local in nature, that is, affecting only his or her district or state.

Just as lobbying fellow colleagues for a seat on a particular committee offers a means to a desired end, so will a member successfully obtain a hearing on his or her bill through constant communication with the membership. Obviously, membership on the committee to which one's bill is referred helps, especially if the chairperson expresses an interest in the legislation. Also, circulation of a "Dear Colleague" letter to the 434 other House or 99 Senate offices in an effort to find cosponsors will publicize and promote the legislation. Press conferences help, too. At the beginning of the 104th Congress, legislation to implement the provisions in the House Republicans' election manifesto, the Contract with America, has received immediate hearings by committees in the House of Representatives. The promise to vote on all measures in the contract during the first 100 days of the 104th Congress was taken seriously by the new chairmen. Media and general interest by the public in change have helped push this agenda forward.

One more interesting way to obtain a hearing is by involving the executive branch, which in the twentieth century has greatly influenced the legislative agenda on the Hill. The influence and power exerted from the White House can be the best way to ensure that a hearing will or will not occur.

If a chairperson agrees to hold a hearing, he and his staff draw up a list of witnesses to appear before the committee. Witnesses who favor or oppose the legislation can come from any number of sources. Individuals with a certain area of expertise or reputation, such as Henry Kissinger, a former secretary of state, are invited to appear alone. For the most part, however, panels of three or four witnesses with similar views testify together. In the case of the impact of new immigration policy, elected state, local, and county officials testified as a group on Capitol Hill. If the issue is environmental in nature, representatives from the Fish and Wildlife Federation, Friends of the Earth, and the Wilderness Society may form a panel. A 5-minute summary of the testimony is usually read at the time of the hearing. Members of the committee then are each given a certain amount of time to question the witnesses. Usually, the more senior members of the majority party begin the questioning.

Since most of the committee work on Capitol Hill takes place on Tuesday, Wednesday, and Thursday, the committee staff makes sure that the "best" witnesses appear early in the week or even early in a session of Congress. The consideration of proposed amendments to the Constitution in the area of social policy (e.g., prayer in the schools, busing, and anti-abortion) during the early 1980s provides an example of the chairperson's power. Rep. Peter Rodino of New Jersey, then chairperson of the House Judiciary Committee, opposed these proposed amendments. He proceeded to hold hearings on these amendments and invited hundreds of witnesses to testify before the committee over a period of 14 months without ever calling for a vote. This power of scheduling by a chairperson illustrates well where much authority is held on Capitol Hill. In contrast to the Democrats, the Republican-controlled Judiciary Committee in the House held numerous hearings and voted out two constitutional amendments and 19 bills within the first 60 days of the 104th Congress.

Frequently, witnesses and citizens are disappointed when only one or two members of a committee are present to listen to testimony. However, the testimony itself, which must be submitted to the committee at least 24 hours in advance of the hearing, is read by the staff and sometimes by the members and is included in the committee transcript. Since so much information is given out in advance and because of demanding schedules, members of a committee often do not feel compelled to attend a hearing. However, if the press and television news cameras are scheduled to cover a hearing, attendance is usually quite high.

Under the House rules, the presence of two members of a committee or a subcommittee constitutes a quorum for congressional hearings that take place to gather testimony. Depending on a committee's rules, one-third of the committee must be present to take up amendments and other business. To report a bill out of committee, a majority of the members must be present. In the Senate, where nearly every Republican senator chairs at least one committee or subcommittee, only one member of the majority party must be present for a hearing to be held.

After the public hearings have been completed, the public markup takes place. It is at this time that changes in the legislation are made. Committee members along with the committee's staff review the bill title by title, line by line, and word for word. Members who wish to offer amendments do so. Very much aware of the presence of lobbying groups, executive branch personnel, and some citizenry, they cast their votes for or against the proposed changes. These mark-up sessions are where the interest groups and the administration find committee members who are willing to sponsor amendments that will promote their causes.

Under the new rules in the Republican-controlled House of Representatives, proxy voting can no longer take place in committee or subcommittee. In addition, all votes on bills and amendments in committee will be published, and all hearings will be open to the public. Finally, the procedure of a "rolling quorum" — holding open a committee vote indefinitely — that had been practiced by the Democrats has also been eliminated.

Rarely are these amendments overturned by the committee or on the House or Senate floor. Complaints of too much congressional power abiding in subcommittee have some validity. Powerful interest groups with the dollars and technology to generate huge mailings from voters in a member's district or home state have greatly affected the environment on the Hill and the way business is conducted. The combination of an effective lobbying contact in Washington with a sense of the political pulse of the state and district has had a tremendous effect on the U.S. Congress, an institution still sensitive to the voters back home.

If the full committee considers a piece of legislation and votes to accept it, the staff then prepares a committee report to accompany the bill. The report is very important for it serves to a great extent as the bill's legislative history, providing guidance to those who will be responsible for implementing its terms. It is also the document that most members read, rather than reading the legislation. Finally, it must accompany the bill for floor consideration.

This last requirement is often used by a chairperson who opposes a bill that was voted favorably out of his or her committee. Staff can be ordered to take months to write the report. This tactic could effectively kill the bill, since Congress may adjourn before a vote on the bill is taken.

Oversight Hearings

Nowhere is the evidence more obvious that Congress is reviewer and deliberator than in the exercise of its oversight function in committees. As the legislative branch, Congress makes laws while the executive branch implements them. As the funding source of programmatic legislation, Congress feels that it has the right to review or investigate the activities of departments and agencies in the executive branch.

The activities of the Committee on Governmental Affairs in the Senate and the Committee on Government Reform and Oversight in the House concentrate on investigating areas of waste and inefficiency that may exist in federal agencies. The authorization for funding the General Accounting Office, the investigative "watchdog" of the Congress, comes from these committees. There are also subcommittees, such as the Subcommittee on the Internal Revenue Service of the Senate Finance Committee and the subcommittees on oversight and investigation of several House committees, whose work is primarily that of review, oversight, and investigation. Furthermore, all standing committees on Capitol Hill have oversight responsibilities. Authorizing committees have the power to "deauthorize" federal programs if on review they are found unsuccessful or inefficient. Appropriations committees can refuse to refund programs, thereby making them unable to operate.

Investigation Hearings

Oversight hearings often can lead to investigative reviews. In fact, the line between these two activities is quite fine. Investigation hearings take place when a review of an agency's activities suggests that something illegal has taken place. Such hearings have increased in the 1980s mostly because of the growth of federal laws and regulations, which affect voters more than ever, and huge budget deficits, which have led to greater scrutiny of federal programs.

Congressional review of the Iran-Contra affair during the 100th Congress best illustrates investigative hearings. Although a joint committee of senators and representatives conducted the Iran-Contra investigation, there have been instances when several committees have pursued an agenda because of a questionable issue. For example, as many as six committees in the House called special hearings in 1983 at which the Environmental Protection Agency's administrator, Ann Burford Gorsuch, appeared and was "grilled." These probings resulted in her resignation and the conviction and jailing of her deputy, Rita Lavelle, who oversaw the Superfund. Committees in the 101st Congress called for extensive investigation of the Federal Savings and Loan Insurance Corporation in the wake of the catastrophic failures of savings and loan companies across the country. And finally, the 103rd Congress held several hearings on the Whitewater affair involving President Clinton and his wife.

Confirmation Hearings

Only the Senate holds confirmation hearings. Serving as a kind of "ad hoc" oversight function, the panels seek to review the past activities of future cabinet secretaries, ambassadors, and Supreme Court justices who have been nominated by the President. Some of these hearings go smoothly, as in the case of William Perry's nomination and confirmation as secretary of the defense during the 103rd Congress. However, in a prior Congress with the same Democratic majority in the Senate, the Judiciary Committee failed to recommend the nomination of Robert Bork to the Supreme Court. During the 101st Congress, President Bush nominated former Sen. John Tower to be secretary of defense, but the Senate refused to confirm the nomination.

SUMMARY

Some people argue that the hearing process is so well orchestrated that not much takes place in a useful, substantive way. However, it is important to remember that these hearings do occur, and they are open to the public. America has a representative and not a parliamentary government. Superseding the political party agenda are the interests of constituents and the lobbying groups that represent many of them. These interests are of chief concern to members of Congress when they serve on committees.

CHAPTER 5
Congressional Staff on Capitol Hill

One of the greatest changes on Capitol Hill in the past 25 years has been the growth of congressional staff. In 1960, about 6,000 people worked for the representatives and senators. Congressional reforms in the 1970s increased the work force in Congress to more than 20,000. With the 1994 congressional elections which resulted in a Republican-controlled Congress in 1995, congressional staff has been cut by one-third. Now about 16,000 people work as personal and committee staff, police, and maintenance personnel as well as staff for the congressional agencies, those being, the Congressional Research Service (CRS), General Accounting Office (GAO), Congressional Budget Office (CBO), and Office of Technology Assessment (OTA).

Over the years, many members of Congress have felt that there are too many staff and too many eager, young people who generate more work. Even though greater staffing expanded the lawmakers' expertise in a broader range of legislative issue areas, in an effort to save money and reduce the size of government, the 104th Congress is determined to cut the size of the staff. Since the voters have asked for less government at the federal level, arguments that the voters and the country as a whole are better served because of greater staff support no longer prevail.

However, more aides working for a representative or senator, whether personal or committee staff, also means more opportunity for access to a member of Congress. Most contact with the elected officials on Capitol Hill occurs through interaction with their staffs. Members of Congress are too busy to meet with everyone about legislative issues or constituents' problems.

Knowing congressional staff on all levels — from caseworkers to administrative assistants — and developing relationships with them are key to working with the Congress (see chart on p. 67).

PROFILE OF CONGRESSIONAL STAFFERS

The reasons why people want to work on Capitol Hill vary as greatly as the 540 members of Congress they serve. Power, influence, and self-promotion, even a sense of place in history for some, explain what motivates many people to work very long hours in very cramped offices.

The rights and privileges of congressional staff depend on their relationship with the member of Congress for whom they work. Until the 104th Congress, workplace laws that applied to the private sector and the federal executive and judiciary branches of government did not apply to Capitol Hill. A staffer could be fired on the spot with no recourse. Although Congress passes laws that affect employer-employee relationships for most Americans, until recently, it remained exempt from the legalities of equal employment and affirmative action.

In October 1988, however, representatives in the House voted overwhelmingly to grant protection under the Civil Rights Act of 1964 to the more than 12,000 persons who work for them. The Office of Fair Employment Practices (OFEP) was established to air employees' complaints. The Senate eventually followed the House's lead, creating an OFEP in 1992.

These offices were meant to function in a similar fashion to the Equal Employment Opportunity Commission and other executive branch enforcement agencies, but they were never really that active.

At the beginning of the 104th Congress, lawmakers passed

Legislative Staff and Agencies

Support Agencies

- Congressional Research Service
- General Accounting Office
- Office of Technology Assessment
- Congressional Budget Office

Committee Staff

- Staff Director
- General Counsel
- Professional Committee Staff
- Administrative Staff

Member's Personal Staff

- Administrative Assistant/Chief of Staff
- Executive Secretary
- Legislative Assistants
- Caseworkers
- State/District Office Staff

the Congressional Accountability Act that applies nearly a dozen private-sector laws to Congress. Among those included are the Civil Rights Act and Age Discrimination and Rehabilitation Act as well as the Family and Medical Leave Act, the Fair Labor Standards Act, and the Occupational Safety and Health Act (OSHA). By 1996, most of the 11 laws will go into effect on Capitol Hill.

The low pay and the willingness to work a 60- to 70-hour week with little job protection or promise of promotion suggest that many of the Capitol Hill staff are young. Burnout is so great that the average tenure of service in Congress is only 4 years. The accountability of the elected officials for whom they work remains foremost in their minds. Whether personal staff or committee staff, these people could lose their jobs if the member who hired them is defeated. Many Democratic Senate staffers who served as committee staff for years found themselves unemployed after the 1994 election when the Republicans won control of the House and the Senate.

Always conscious of the scrutiny and power of the voters and interest groups, congressional staff are generally courteous and cordial, return phone calls, and try to help, despite the pressures of their jobs. Their willingness or reluctance to serve as an extension of the legislator can affect positively or negatively the public's perception of the elected official.

TYPES OF STAFF ON CAPITOL HILL

There are three categories of staff on the Hill. Generally speaking, *personal staff* assist a member in the role of representative while the *committee staff* serve the members in their roles as policymakers. Personal staff work in each of the offices of the 540 representatives and senators. Committee staff, generally older, more educated, and professional, provide input and expertise for legislation drafted by more than 200 committees and subcommittees. Finally, those who work at CRS, GAO, OTA, and CBO serve as key *information staff,* usually behind the scenes, for the Congress in all constituent-related and legislative areas.

Personal Staff

The office of each member operates differently. The atmosphere and work schedule depend totally on how the representative or senator chooses to run his or her office. Usually, every office in both the House and Senate has an *administrative assistant* (the "AA"), several *legislative assistants, caseworkers,* an *executive secretary,* and *district office staff.*

Administrative Assistant

The AA, sometimes called the chief of staff, ranks highest among staff in the Washington office of an elected official. He or she confers with the member in hiring office staff, setting salary levels, and delegating workload. Usually the AA is quite close with the member, knowing well the political pulse and profile of the district or state. An appointment with an AA is nearly like meeting with the representative or senator personally.

Legislative Assistants

A legislative assistant, or LA, usually focuses on particular policy issues, such as energy or health. The duties include keeping the member abreast of developments in a specific area, serving as a liaison with the committee staff handling that topic (especially if the member sits on that committee), handling constituent mail concerning the issue, and meeting with lobbyists and voters as the member's personal representative for the issue of concern.

Caseworkers

Caseworkers resolve problems and answer inquiries from constituents. A knowledge of federal agencies and departments is required for their job, which can be largely that of finding lost Social Security checks and solving problems with veterans' retirement benefits. Successful constituency service can be measured by these individuals' activities, which include assistance in federal grant applications for a district and publicity for the member if the grant is awarded. Increasingly, caseworkers have been placed in the district offices where they are able to deal directly and more personally with constituents' problems.

Press Secretary

This congressional staffer serves as the member's chief spokesperson to the media, writes press releases, and organizes press conferences. If citizens, interest groups, or federal agencies wish to promote their special issue, they direct newsletters, correspondence, and reports to this aide.

Executive Secretary

Executive secretaries can be among the most important people in terms of gaining access to an elected official. These personal staff aides make the appointments and juggle the members' unpredictable schedules.

District/State Offices

Every representative to the House has at least one office in his or her district; each senator has several offices to serve his or her state. These offices, often located in a federal building, work directly on the local problems of constituents and increasingly are handling casework for the members. Located in the home area, close to the voters, these offices respond directly to the voters of the district or state.

These are the people to work with if a citizens' group or association wishes to invite its lawmaker to speak or participate in a local conference. A personal tour of a local medical facility, school, or factory can help considerably in promoting desired legislation. If the elected official cannot accept an invitation, the director of the district office may attend instead.

PERSONAL STAFF IN THE HOUSE AND THE SENATE

Each of the 440 members of the House of Representatives is allowed to have a paid staff of no more than 18 full-time and four part-time employees to serve in both the Washington and district offices. The total amount of money each year for the salaries of these staffers is $568,560. Most representatives return some of this money at the end of each year and often do not hire all of the staff to which they are entitled. The average salary of a personal staffer in the House is $35,510.

Many of these people are just out of college or graduate school, aggressive, ambitious, and eager to serve the member well while, at the same time, promoting themselves, often seeming somewhat arrogant. One former Hill staffer, who went to work in the congressional liaison office of a federal department, commented, "I never realized how obnoxious and abrasive we appeared to be until I left the Hill. Now when I call a member's office on behalf of the executive branch agency, I am often shocked by the cockiness of the staffers in the members' offices, many of whom I know are much younger than I." On the whole, however, most of these people try to respond as quickly and as best as they can to requests made by the public and especially by the district.

When a representative is first elected to Congress, all of the staff in Washington may come from the district. Often these loyal campaign workers, who served the nominee well back home, find life in Washington too expensive or inhospitable and soon return home, perhaps to serve in a district office. Of course, members try to have staff who are from the district, especially for the AA position. However, experienced caseworkers whose members were defeated in the November elections can often find jobs in new members' offices because they know the federal agencies well and realize the value of accurate and timely response to constituent needs.

Responding to constituent mail has become more important

than ever on Capitol Hill. With the growth of the federal government and its extension into people's lives, the representatives increasingly play the role of "ombudsman" for their constituents. In the complex American society of the late twentieth century, the representative is the U.S. government for many of the voters in his or her district. A quick resolution to the problem of a student loan payment or a stolen passport for one voter can mean more votes in the next election as the news spreads among friends and neighbors that "our representative in Washington took care of my problem with the government."

In summary, the personal staff of a member of the House of Representatives exists to work for the reelection of the member whose defeat would mean the loss of their own jobs. As a result, these people work hard to serve and respond to the needs of the district.

The Senate rules on the number of personal staff differ from those of the House. Since each senator represents an entire state, a Senate office budget for staff hiring depends on the state's population. The senators of California may each have a staff of 75, while Sen. Joseph Biden of Delaware may have only 35. In addition to the administrative assistant and legislative assistants, there is often a director of legislative affairs in a senator's office whose job is to coordinate the senator's legislative positions and program.

Most senators have several state offices where nearly all of the caseworkers on his or her staff are located. Although responsive to constituent needs, the senator, representing an entire state for 6 years, does not have the closeness with the voters that a representative has who is up for reelection every 2 years.

Because of the size of a senator's personal staff, aides often do not even know the senator much less have any kind of personal rapport, as often exists in the House.

COMMITTEE STAFF ON CAPITOL HILL

The people whose primary job is to assist the representatives and senators in their jobs as legislators are the committee staff on Capitol Hill. Even with the reforms in the House of Representatives for the 104th Congress that have reduced the number of committees in that chamber, there are still more than 200 committees and subcommittees on Capitol Hill. In further efforts for reform and to save money, both the House and the Senate have reduced by one-third the size of their committee staffs in 1995.

On the whole, the committee staff are older, more educated, and more professional than the personal staff. Many of these people have law degrees or advanced degrees in specialized areas such as tax, economics, or engineering. Some staff have left careers in the executive branch, such as the Navy, the National Park Service, or the Forest Service. They provide the lawmakers with substantive information and background for proposed legislation. Some of them actually draft the bills and resolutions proposed by lobbying groups, the administration, or by the members themselves. Until the 1994 congressional elections when the Republicans won control of the House for the first time in 40 years, there were Democratic committee staffers in the House and the Senate that had worked on the same committee or subcommittee for nearly 20 years. Such long tenure of service made these committee aides the source of legislative history and background on programs in the face of a changing Congress, half of whose Senate is serving its first term and over half of whose House has been elected since 1990. Because these committee positions are not permanent, the Republican capture of the Congress in 1994 has brought many new staffers to the committees who have not worked on Capitol Hill before.

Depending on a committee's rules and budget, the chairperson and members of a subcommittee hire and fire the staff who work for them. Controversy can arise over a subcommittee's budget for staff hiring, especially when the chairperson of the full committee is powerful and at odds with a subcommittee chairperson. In the 104th Congress there is general agreement on both sides of Capitol Hill that committees' budgets will be lower and they are due to reduction in the size of staff.

Most of the committees have both a majority staff and a separate minority staff. Having greater power because they are the majority, the Republican committee staffers in the House and in the Senate play larger roles in setting the legislative agendas. They also advise the committee members during the hearings and mark-up sessions, and assist in the floor debate during final consideration of a bill.

Promotion of legislation and access to the committee members are possible through contact with the committee staff. The *staff director* and the *general counsel* could be described as the political staff — those people who are closely allied with the chairperson and work with interest groups, committee staffers on the other side of the Hill, and agency officials to facilitate or obstruct the passage of legislation.

The *professional staff* provide the expertise essential for drafting legislation. As policy specialists in a particular area, these aides suggest alternatives to a legislative measure, often as a means of compromise with the House or the wishes of the administration.

The *administrative staff* arrange the hearing rooms, organize the office and publications, and oversee the committee's budget and expenses.

Finally, most committees have a *press secretary* who writes news releases on a committee's agenda to encourage and promote media coverage of hearings, both on Capitol Hill and in the congressional districts across the country.

LEGISLATIVE SUPPORT AGENCIES

Another group of staff serving the members of Congress are those people who work for CRS, GAO, CBO, and OTA. As additional sources of information for legislation and investigation for the senators and representatives, the professional staff of these agencies offer expertise in just about all areas of public policy, from MX missiles to taxes to the savings and loan crisis to environmental studies. Unlike the personal and committee staff aides, these professional staff are nonpartisan and are hired to give objective advice and information to any member of Congress who makes a request.

Congressional Research Service

Established originally in 1914 as the Legislative Reference Service for the Library of Congress, CRS employs about 400 professional staff who respond to thousands of inquiries and requests from the Congress each year. Having the resources of the Library of Congress at their disposal (the best and largest depository of its kind in the world), the CRS staff provide the elected officials as well as the congressional committees with information needed to draft, review, or investigate legislation. As the expertise and reputation of its staff have grown, CRS has been increasingly called on to offer in-depth analysis and review of issues to committees.

General Accounting Office

The largest of the support agencies, employing more than 4,000 people, the GAO was created in 1921 with the passage of the Budget and Accounting Act. Known as the "watchdog" of the Congress, this agency reviews and audits the operations of programs implemented by executive branch agencies established by the Congress. During the years of tighter fiscal constraints, its role of investigation and oversight grew. Originally employing only accountants, GAO now hires hundreds of other professionals such as scientists, physicians, economists, and business management experts. On site investigations of executive branch activities in Washington, across the country, and around the world are either self-initiated or at the request of members of Congress. The comptroller general of the United States, Charles A. Bowsher, directs this agency, reports of which frequently provide Congress with information challenging the activities and operation of the executive branch.

Office of Technology Assessment

Reforms in the 104th Congress have promoted the abolition of the Office of Technology Assessment to save money. As the smallest of the congressional support agencies, the OTA employs about 125 full-time staff. It provides the Congress with scientific reports on the long-term physical, chemical, and biological effects of various technological developments. Much of the research for the reports on the OTA projects is contracted out to scientists, engineers, and other highly and specially trained professionals.

Congressional Budget Office

The newest of the congressional support agencies, CBO was established in 1974 with the passage of the Budget and Impoundment Control Act. Employing about 230 people, its reputation for excellence in budget and economic matters has grown steadily over the past decade. Working primarily for the budget, tax, and appropriations committees of the House and Senate, CBO's economists and fiscal specialists analyze economic data, make projections on the national budget deficit, and provide the lawmakers with information as they work on the federal budget.

Acting only in an advisory capacity, CBO offers Congress the budgetary and economic expertise that the Office of Management and Budget (OMB) provides the President. Increasingly controversial during the Reagan administration, CBO has projected deficits and economic downturns contrary to what the directors of OMB have predicted. This office also projected in 1994 that the health care plan proposed by the Clinton administration was not affordable.

SUMMARY

It cannot be denied that the influence and power of staff on Capitol Hill have grown in the past 20 years. Their crucial role as conduits of information to the elected officials is a vital element in making public policy on Capitol Hill. As Congress reduces the size of staff to save money, it also reduces its sources of information. This may mean a greater reliance on federal agency staff, lobbyists, and think tanks.

CHAPTER 6
The President As Legislator

The President's power to veto legislation passed by the Congress as well as his need to seek the advice and consent of the Senate to ratify treaties with foreign countries have always been felt on Capitol Hill. However, twentieth century Presidents have increasingly taken a more active role in the legislative process.

U.S. Presidents in this century, believing that they represent all of the American people, have established themselves more in congressional activities by initiating and orchestrating a legislative agenda for Capitol Hill to act on. New Freedom, New Deal, New Frontier, and Reaganomics are names of presidential legislative programs that became the slogans of various administrations. This chapter will examine the evolution of the President as legislator in the following ways: greater familiarity with Capitol Hill, development of a lobbying staff within the White House and the executive agencies, and control over the national budget.

THE CHIEF EXECUTIVE AND CAPITOL HILL

George Washington and John Adams complied with Article II, Section 3, of the Constitution by personally giving the State of the Union address before both houses of the Congress. Our third President, Thomas Jefferson, was a very ineffective public speaker and rather than deliver the speech himself he had it read before Congress. The separation of powers in legislative matters was evident for more than a century.

It was not until Woodrow Wilson, a historian who knew the tradition of the first two Presidents, that the President once again returned to Capitol Hill to review with Congress the state of the union and to outline a legislative program. This physical presence of the chief executive within the halls of Congress meant a greater involvement of the President in the legislative process.

Almost every President since Wilson has gone to Capitol Hill at times other than the delivery of the State of the Union address to promote his legislative programs. In fact, not all of the twentieth century Presidents have been unknown within the halls of Congress. Eight of the 18 presidents since 1900 served on Capitol Hill.

However, being a former member of the House of Representatives or Senate has not necessarily ensured that a legislative program passed easily through the Congress. Some Presidents who were total outsiders to Capitol Hill have had the greatest legislative successes.

Take the cases of Franklin D. Roosevelt and Ronald Reagan, former governors. Neither of these men had ever been elected to Congress, yet each of them had incredible legislative victories on the Hill. During the now famous "first 100 days" of the Roosevelt administration in 1933, Congress passed major pieces of legislation proposed by Roosevelt.

In the spring and summer of 1981, Ronald Reagan implemented his Reaganomics program, even with a Republican minority in the House of Representatives. Reagan managed to unite the conservative Democrats with the Republicans in the House to defeat the Democrats on the budget and tax bills. Reagan knew how to court elected officials for a vote.

Another former governor, Jimmy Carter, did not fare so well. Having run for the office of President in the wake of the Watergate scandal and against the Washington establishment, Carter did not see the importance of seeking the cooperation and the advice of the Democratic leaders on Capitol Hill to carry out his legislative program. Too concerned with the details and the "rightness" of his legislative package rather than with the interests and the personalities of the lawmakers themselves, Carter had an extremely difficult time on the Hill, even with a Democratic majority in both the House and the Senate.

Both John F. Kennedy and Lyndon B. Johnson had served in Congress, but Johnson was far more successful in getting the Civil Rights Bill of 1964 and the Great Society programs through Congress. Some analysts say that the congressional opposition to his programs that Kennedy had encountered was beginning to turn around at the time of his assassination.

Like Kennedy, Johnson had served in the House and Senate, but Johnson had been majority leader in the Senate. He knew well the strategies of the legislative process and how to use them on certain members of Congress at crucial times. He felt comfortable meeting with the powerful committee chairpersons of both the House and the Senate to seek their advice while at the same time convincing them to vote with him.

Today, with the diffusion of power among the more than 200 committee and subcommittee chairpersons, the personal touches and interviews of a Johnson-style presidency are all that more difficult to achieve. However, major victories are still possible on Capitol Hill. The legislative successes of Ronald Reagan during his first year of office reflect his warm and personable style, a stark contrast to Carter's colder and technical approach. Combining good personal rapport with a well-organized and well-managed Office of Congressional Relations, Ronald Reagan achieved significant legislative victories on Capitol Hill.

George Bush, a former House member, continued the more personal style of Reagan and in a less confrontational way than his predecessor. By inviting members of Congress to informal gatherings in the first family's living quarters, Bush tried to maintain a positive, open-door relationship with the legislative branch. Different budget priorities between the Bush White House and the Democrat-controlled Congress contributed to the breakdown of congressional relations that began so well.

As an outsider to Washington, D.C., Bill Clinton met with unusually high legislative successes during the first session of the 103rd Congress, largely because of the Democrat-controlled Congress. Despite the fact that the Democratics controlled both the legislative and executive branches of government, however, Clinton's controversial health care plan failed to pass during the second session of the 103rd Congress.

THE WHITE HOUSE LOBBIES ON CAPITOL HILL

As each twentieth century President's involvement in the legislative process has grown, it naturally followed that an executive branch lobbying staff would develop. During the Eisenhower administration, the Office of Congressional Relations was formally set up in the White House.

In addition to a team of lobbyists whose job over the years has been purely political, Presidents have turned to the legislative affairs staffs in the executive departments and agencies to develop the policy for their legislative programs and to assist in legislative liaison on the Hill.

Congress, often ambivalent about lobbying by the executive branch departments and agencies, has realized over the years that information freely exchanged is vital for the legislative process in a democracy. In fact, the Hill frequently seeks the advice and programmatic expertise of career civil servants.

Dwight Eisenhower to Gerald Ford

It was not until the Eisenhower administration that an office of congressional relations was established in a formal way at the White House. The President wanted such an office not for the purpose of promoting his legislative program on Capitol Hill, but rather to keep the Republican members of Congress who controlled both the House and the Senate in 1952 from asking for political favors from the President.

Lawrence O'Brien, whom John F. Kennedy selected to head the Office of Congressional Relations in 1960, established this office as a lobbying arm for the chief executive. Having worked with Kennedy since 1952, O'Brien knew well the give and take of the political scene. He set the precedent for successful White House liaison with Capitol Hill: political rather than substantive expertise was required of a staff who would build coalitions among the various factions of Congress.

Even though the Democrats controlled both the House and the Senate in 1960, passage of the liberal New Frontier program was not easy. O'Brien recognized and dealt with the political realities of conservative southern Democrats in the House and a minority of northern Democrats in the Senate. Such a philosophical makeup made O'Brien and his team of lobbyists organize along geographical lines rather than on issues.

In addition to organizing a lobbying team that worked directly for the White House, O'Brien also set the precedent for success with Congress by working closely with the executive departments' legislative staffs, the Democratic leadership on the Hill, and the interest groups that favored the President's program. He remained the director of this office under President Lyndon Johnson after Kennedy's death. The combination of his organizational skills with that of LBJ's own political prowess meant the passage of stalled civil rights legislation and the Great Society program.

Richard Nixon and Gerald Ford both knew highs and lows in dealing with the Hill. Nixon frequently expressed his displeasure with Congress and its inability to accomplish its legislative business. Although he had served in the House, the Senate, and as vice president, Nixon did not like the political bargaining that is so vital in working with Capitol Hill. He sometimes bypassed

Information Resources in the Administration and Congress

President | **Congress**

1,300,000 Professional People on Federal Payroll | **17,000 Professional People on Legislative Payroll**

White House Legislative Affairs · White House Office of Public Liaison → **President** ← Cabinet Departments · ◀ Offices of Legislative Affairs ▶ · Executive Branch Agencies

Personal Staff · Committee Staff → **House and Senate 540*** ← Staff from Four Support Agencies

There are five nonvoting delegates in the House from Guam, the Virgin Islands, American Samoa, Puerto Rico, and the District of Columbia.

the legislative process by using executive privilege, as in impounding funds for programs appropriated by Congress.

Bryce Harlow, Clark MacGregor, and William Timmons served as directors of Nixon's Office of Congressional Relations. Conflict between their office and that of Nixon's chief advisers, John Ehrlichman and H. R. Haldeman, did not help promote a legislative program on Capitol Hill. By the beginning of his second term, with Haldeman and Ehrlichman having resigned, Nixon did begin to meet with the Republican congressional leaders on a more regular basis in an effort to cooperate more fully with the Hill.

Gerald Ford's legislative team faced the difficult days following Watergate as well as a Democrat-controlled Congress. Ford chose Max Friedersdorf to lead an Office of Congressional Relations, which played more of a policy-making role during Ford's short administration. Lacking a majority in either house of Congress, Ford's legislative successes on the Hill were exhibited more in blocking veto overrides than implementing legislation.

Jimmy Carter to Bill Clinton

The White House lobbying effort on the Hill continued along geographical lines throughout the Johnson, Nixon, and Ford administrations. Cultivating relationships with certain leading representatives and senators meant a better knowledge of these politicians as people who, as elected officials, had certain district and state needs that had to be kept in mind.

Since Jimmy Carter had run against the Washington establishment in 1976, he did not feel that he owed any allegiance to anyone. Issues of public policy and not the policymakers themselves were more important. As a result, Carter organized his Office of Congressional Relations along issue lines. The director of this office was Frank Moore who, like Carter, was an outsider to Washington and its ways of doing business.

Believing that he could convince the members of Congress

to vote purely on the merits of a piece of legislation without any consideration of projects for a representative's or senator's district or state, Carter never established a good rapport with Congress. Although he had later legislative successes, such as the ratification of the Panama Canal treaties, the "windfall" profits tax on oil companies, and the deregulation of some transportation companies, the perception that Carter's legislative team could not competently deal with Congress remained until the end of his administration.

Ronald Reagan learned from Jimmy Carter's mistakes. Although he had never participated in the Washington scene, Reagan chose Max Friedersdorf, who had worked for Gerald Ford, to head his Office of Congressional Relations. Through the incredible efforts of Friedersdorf and his team of geographically organized lobbyists, President Reagan's legislative program for tax and budget reform was implemented in the summer of 1981. All lobbyists had either congressional or lobbying experience. Although achieving more legislative victories in Reagan's first term than in the second, President Reagan's Office of Congressional Relations had a better relationship and knew greater successes on Capitol Hill than his predecessor's.

George Bush's Office of Congressional Relations, composed of eight professional staff, worked both sides of Capitol Hill. Much legislation, opposed by the President was passed by the Democrat-controlled Congress. As political consensus and comity broke down during the Bush presidency, George Bush successfully vetoed 46 bills.

With the election of Bill Clinton, a Democrat, in 1992 as well as Democratic control of both the House and the Senate during the 103rd Congress for the ensuing 2 years, the White House achieved many legislative successes on Capitol Hill, ranging from deficit reduction to the passage of the North American Free Trade Agreement to the Family Leave Bill. The current director of the White House Office of Legislative Affairs is Patrick J. Griffin, who served as senior floor assistant to then Minority Leader Robert C. Byrd and later as Secretary to the Senate Democrats from 1983 to 1985. With the Republicans in control of both houses of Congress for the 104th Congress, the Clinton White House faces tough opposition on Capitol Hill.

EXECUTIVE AGENCY LIAISON WITH CAPITOL HILL

The offices of legislative affairs in the departments and agencies throughout the executive branch work with the White House domestic policy staff, a group of counselors who develop a legislative agenda strictly for national issues. These agencies work for the chief executive whose legislative agenda they must support. These legislative offices are legally forbidden to participate in or promote a grass-roots lobby of voters to pressure members of Congress on a piece of legislation. In a society where the free exchange of information is related to the open and democratic process, the line between public relations or department liaison and outright lobbying can be a fine one. Many departments, such as the Navy, the Army, and the Office of Personnel Management, have offices of legislative affairs in the House and Senate office buildings. Thus, their staffs can educate representatives, senators, and their staffs about various programs.

The executive departments' legislative affairs staffs also work closely with the White House Office of Congressional Relations and domestic policy counsels to coordinate legislation and to encourage a single, united effort and voice for the administration. Frequently headed by political appointees (Schedule Cs) who have Hill contacts, these legislative affairs offices draw on the knowledge and expertise of thousands of career civil servants in designing policy for the President's legislative program.

The strong inducement of the executive branch in crafting the makeup of legislative affairs staffs has been vital to a strong voice on the Hill. Jimmy Carter chose to let the department's secretary appoint his or her own legislative staffs. As a result, some people in his administration felt that an agency's liaison staff worked more for their department's programs than for the administration as a whole. The single voice from the executive branch, with the White House Office of Congressional Relations directing the administration's efforts on Capitol Hill, often came across as a chorus during the Carter years.

Office of Public Liaison

Although Carter had difficulties maintaining a unity of legislative effort between the White House and the executive departments, he did create the Office of Public Liaison to lobby lobbyists. Directed by Anne Wexler, this office exerted grassroots pressure on members of Congress by seeking the assistance of public and private interest groups who legally could encourage voters to write or call their senator or representative.

The influence and use of computers in the political process have opened up access by the public to the politician and have led to massive lobbying campaigns. Literally millions of cards and letters flooded Capitol Hill during the spring and summer of 1981 when lobbying groups reached the voters to push for President Reagan's economic plan of budget and tax cuts. Through the efforts of this Office of Public Liaison, directed by Elizabeth Dole, thousands of lobbying groups from across the country were contacted to encourage voters to pressure their representatives and senators into supporting the President's new economic plan.

THE PRESIDENT AND THE NATIONAL BUDGET

Reagan won legislative victories in the areas of budget and tax not only because of his popularity and successful lobbying. The evolution and influence of the office of the President in this century has meant a greater role for the President as manager of the entire government. As the leading "executive" officer, he should have input into the makeup of the national budget.

Article I, Section 7, of the Constitution clearly states that revenue-raising legislation begins in the House of Representatives. However, congressional response to an executive branch legislative agenda involving the areas of budget and tax has become the way of lawmaking in this century.

When the House established the Committee on Ways and Means as a permanent committee in 1794, it provided itself with an institutional means to oversee the national purse. Over the next 100 years (with the exception of the Civil War), the Congress remained the dominant branch of government, controlling the business of the state through tariffs and tax measures. With the development in the 1820s of today's system of standing committees on the Hill, the President's influence in the legislative process weakened. Power in the Congress was diffused among the committee chairpersons, each of whom had his own legislative agenda.

Such diffusion of power through the committee system, while strengthening the Congress in the nineteenth century, has weakened it today because the executive branch has an authority and stature that it did not have 100 years ago.

Between 1870 and 1920, the United States was involved in and won two wars, the Spanish-American War and World War I. As commander-in-chief during these crises, the President's stature grew along with governmental services and expenditures. The number of executive departments and agencies grew, and it was gradually felt by the lawmakers on Capitol Hill that the President as chief executive should oversee the operations and budgets of these bureaus to have a more responsible government.

In 1921 Congress passed the Budget and Accounting Act, the purpose of which was to control agency spending. Each department would be required to submit a projected budget to the

Bureau of the Budget (BOB) at the Department of the Treasury. The BOB would make changes and the President would then submit these budgets to Congress for approval. As originally conceived, the 1921 act was not perceived by Congress to lessen its power over the national budget.

However, Franklin D. Roosevelt saw government's role differently when his New Deal legislation created even more agencies and regulations for the country. Believing that larger government should indeed be a permanent part of America's future, he moved the BOB from the Department of the Treasury to the executive office of the President. By establishing direct White House control over the government's budget, the President would then propose a legislative program on Capitol Hill for Congress to fund executive branch activities. Thus began the Congress's role of responding to rather than initiating budget requests.

SUMMARY

The President of the United States is involved more than ever before in the legislative process on Capitol Hill. His term of 4 years is twice as long as that of any one member of the House of Representatives, all of whose members are up for re-election every 2 years. The growth in the size, strength, and stability of the executive office of the President in this century has enabled it to bridge the gap between the executive and legislative branches of government. Such efficiency by the executive branch has not, however, evolved into an executive tyranny, because in this country the nation's leader still must answer to the inefficient but watchful other end of Pennsylvania Avenue, Capitol Hill.

CHAPTER 7
The Federal Budget and the Congressional Budget Process

In 1974 Congress passed the Budget and Impoundment Control Act in an effort to influence the course and content of the national budget. Reacting to the power of the "imperial presidencies" of Lyndon B. Johnson and Richard Nixon as well as negative public opinion toward Washington in the wake of the Vietnam conflict and Watergate, the lawmakers on Capitol Hill felt that the legislative branch needed to reassert its constitutional right to control the country's purse strings. Responding to presidential initiatives, especially in budget matters, and not proposing its own throughout the 1960s had eroded the power of Congress over the budget. In the years prior to 1974, power was only in a few places on Capitol Hill, thus enabling the White House to deal with only a few members, particularly senior members of Congress, to pass its programs.

During the years when the economics of deficit spending was the national way of government business, both for Republican and Democratic presidents, there were no committees on the Hill monitoring the bottom line of expenditures versus revenues. Programs were created by the authorizing committees, funded by the appropriations committees, and implemented by the executive branch with little regard for tax revenues to pay for the government's services. Along with this near automatic budget approval process on Capitol Hill, both the Johnson and Nixon administrations oversaw the creation of new entitlement programs, which meant greater government spending for people's needs. Johnson's Great Society initiatives such as Medicare and Medicaid, and President Nixon's entitlement programs of General Revenue Sharing, the Comprehensive Employment and Training Act, and Community Development exemplify the chief executive's legislative successes on Capitol Hill in those years, victories that meant greater government spending. It was not until the passage of the Budget Act in 1974 that Congress established "tally sheets" to consider the budget.

The lack of institutional means to oversee the budget combined with the impoundment of funds by Nixon led concerned lawmakers to conceive and pass the Budget Act of 1974. The act made these changes:

- The fiscal year (FY) would begin on October 1 rather than July 1 to give Congress more time to study and discuss the budget.
- House and Senate budget committees would be established to set economic priorities by making spending recommendations to the appropriations and revenue-raising (tax) committees, thereby imposing a discipline on the budgeting process.
- The Congressional Budget Office (CBO) would be created to provide Congress with data and objective in-house advice for spending and taxes. (CBO serves Congress in much the same manner as the Office of Management and Budget [OMB] serves the President.)
- Congress would have the right to review and approve proposed presidential impoundment of funds.
- Congress would follow a timetable for budget passage.

Nearly two decades have passed since Congress began working within the guidelines of the budget process. What this process is, how it has changed in the past 17 years, and how it works will be outlined on the following pages.

THE FEDERAL BUDGET AND THE EXECUTIVE BRANCH

The formulation of the President's budget begins about 19 months before the fiscal year under consideration. This means that in March 1995, the executive branch began planning for the 1997 budget, which takes effect on October 1, 1996.

Each year in the late winter and early spring, bureaucrats in the executive branch's agencies and departments submit their requests to their program and budget offices for activities they wish to be funded. After many months of negotiations among the White House, OMB, and the agencies, the President's budget is submitted to Capitol Hill in early February of each year.

If the United States had a parliamentary form of government, approval of the budget by the legislative branch would be immediate. The chief executive in parliamentary government holds his position because he is the leader of the party that has the majority of seats in the lawmaking body of the government. Under this system, however, there is no separation of powers between the executive and legislative branches like that which exists in the United States.

The Constitution calls for the legislative branch to be the revenue-raising arm of the government. Over the years, Congress has become very involved in the appropriating process. Thus, a federal budget that is submitted to Capitol Hill with the politics and legislative agenda of one individual behind it, the President, encounters the legislative agendas and parochial interests of the 540 members of Congress.

CONGRESSIONAL BUDGET PROCESS

The guidelines established by the 1974 Budget Act called for a series of steps that, at the time, included procedures that would set total budget targets for the next fiscal year. The process laid out a series of date-specific deadlines, starting in March and ending in September, for the lawmakers to meet in budget considerations over a 6-month period.

For the first few fiscal years following 1974, Congress kept to its timetable. The members in both houses of Congress took the schedule quite seriously. Even Sen. John Stennis, who in the mid-1970s was chairperson of both the Senate Armed Services Committee and the Defense Subcommittee on Appropriations, was made to comply with the dates and spending ceilings set by the Senate Budget Committee.

The process did not work well or smoothly in the face of growing deficits in the 1980s. Congress, which established this timetable, could ignore it, and this was exactly what happened. With no budget in place by October 1, the government was funded by continuing resolution.

This last-minute scramble led to government shutdowns in recent years, and greatly frustrated executive branch planners whose projects could not be implemented because Congress had not voted the money for the programs.

In an effort to gain better control over the mounting deficit, Congress passed the Balanced Budget and Emergency Deficit Control Act, which President Ronald Reagan signed on December 12, 1985. The act called for the budget deficit, then $171.9 billion, to be reduced annually beginning with FY 1986, the goal being to eliminate the deficit by FY 1991. Reflecting the general sentiment that Congress lacks the political will to curb deficits through the processes created by the 1974 Budget and Impoundment Control Act, the new legislation included mandatory cuts to balance the budget by October 1990.

The Gramm-Rudman-Hollings bill, which was named for the three senators who sponsored it, monopolized much of the legislative agenda in the fall of 1985. It was originally offered as an amendment to a bill to raise the nation's debt ceiling to $2.079 trillion from $1.824 trillion. Failure to pass the bill by December 12, 1985, would have caused the United States to default for the first time in its history.

The highlights of the Gramm-Rudman-Hollings Act included: the goal of $0 in deficits for FY 1991; automatic cuts for nonexempt programs to be divided equally between defense and nondefense targets if Congress failed to meet deficit targets in a fiscal year; exemptions from automatic cuts (e.g., Social Security, Medicare, programs for the very poor such as Aid to Families with Dependent Children and food stamps, as well as interest on the national debt); and suspension of automatic cuts in time of war.

On February 7, 1986, a special federal judicial panel in Washington, D.C., declared unconstitutional the automatic budget cutting provision, called sequestration, of the Gramm-Rudman-Hollings budget-balancing law. It violated the Constitution's separation of powers by giving the decision-making power of the executive branch to a legislative branch official, the comptroller general, who is the director of the General Accounting Office (GAO). Since the comptroller general can be removed by Congress, this officer cannot have executive branch decision-making authority. On July 7, 1986, the Supreme Court also ruled that the provision for automatic cuts was unconstitutional.

In the fall of 1987, Congress reinstated the sequestration process (Gramm-Rudman II), but stipulated that automatic cuts should be issued by the President with the recommendation of OMB. Congress also extended the $0 deficit budget goal to FY 1993.

During George Bush's presidency, deficits failed to decline. Conflicts between Capitol Hill and the White House in finding agreement on a budget solution mounted. In an effort to work for more meaningful control over national spending, congressional and presidential budget negotiators finally developed a new process as part of the budget for FY 1991. The 1990 budget agreement called for Congress to pass the Budget Enforcement Act of 1990, which altered the budget process once again.

During fiscal years 1991–1993, the government's discretionary spending (yearly appropriated dollars) was divided among defense, domestic, and international aid programs. Each category was subject to sequestration (automatic cuts) if the money appropriated over the next 3 fiscal years exceeded targets set by the budget agreement reached in the fall of 1990. If a congressional committee wanted to increase spending for any program in these three discretionary areas, cuts had to come from other programs in the category, or revenues had to be raised to fund the new spending through taxes or user fees, a "pay as you go" plan.

In fiscal years 1994 and 1995, the three discretionary spending areas will once again face automatic cuts if the targets for yearly spending are exceeded. This was the original design of Gramm-Rudman-Hollings in 1985.

Exempt from the automatic budget chopping block are the entitlement programs, such as Social Security and Medicare, the fastest growing budget items. However, the "pay as you go" plan will also apply to them. If, for example, a committee wishes to increase Medicare benefits, fees or taxes must be passed to pay for the new benefits. Operation Desert Storm was funded from an account separate from that of defense.

Projection of the programmatic cost estimates as well as the new revenue estimates will rest with OMB, the President's budget office. This task belonged to CBO and the Joint Committee on Taxation, information agents of Congress, before the 1990 budget agreement.

When Bill Clinton was elected president, he promised to halve the budget deficit in his first term. The Omnibus Budget Reconciliation Act of 1993 narrowly passed the 103rd Congress. Containing both spending cuts and tax increases, this plan for deficit reduction continued to freeze the caps for discretionary, appropriated spending, for 5 years, or until 1998. The plan did not call for freezes on any of the entitlement programs. The budget deficit has declined from a record $290 billion in 1992, the last year of George Bush's presidency, to about $250 billion in FY 1994.

As a result of the congressional elections of 1994, the Republican Party gained control of both the House and Senate for the first time in 40 years. Feeling that the American people want less government, the Republicans in the House — guided by their election manifesto, "the Contract with America," that promises a balanced budget by the year 2002 — are determined to cut federal taxes and programs. Republicans in the Senate want to cut spending before taxes. Whichever tactic is taken, President Clinton must sign appropriations bills to fund the national government.

THE FOUR PHASES OF THE BUDGET PROCESS

With the passage of the Budget Enforcement Act in 1990, the 1974 budget process was amended and its timetable was changed (see Appendix A).

Executive Budget Goes to Capitol Hill

Congress reconvenes each January. The President submits his budget request for congressional consideration in early February. With over a year of preparation by the executive branch, the legislative branch now has 9 months to examine and pass the budget. All House and Senate standing committees must submit "views and estimates" of expenditures for the coming year to the budget committees within 6 weeks after the President's submission, the first major deadline in the budget process and also the end of phase one.

Any new program that a department, agency, or lobbying or international group may want funded should be in the President's budget when it is sent to the Hill. Executive agencies along with interest groups have 10 months to try to incorporate funds for their projects into the budget before the President submits his request to Congress. Funding for new projects after the budget has reached the Hill is very difficult to incorporate. Most programs contained in the executive budget and in the committees' February reports to the budget committees will stay in the proposed budget document.

The Budget Resolution

Between late February and April 15, the deadline for passing the budget resolution, the House and Senate budget committees draft their versions of the budget resolution. Desirous of a budget that meets agreed-to targets in both discretionary and entitlement areas, these committees review the standing committees' proposed expenditures, the estimated tax revenues, and the CBO budget analysis to ensure that planned spending conforms to targets set in the 1993 budget agreement. Both houses should pass budget resolutions by April 15, with differences between the two resolved in conference committee. If a budget resolution is not reported by this date, the budget committees set spending limits for appropriations committees in discretionary categories that equal those set in the President's original budget submission.

The Reconciliation Process

The annual budget resolution may contain directions, called reconciliation instructions, that direct certain committees to report legislation that will reduce entitlements, or increase revenues or user fees. They are designed to ensure compliance with the entitlement targets set in the 1993 budget agreement.

Authorization and Appropriation Processes

Most of the work of the House and Senate authorization and appropriations committees takes place between mid-April and mid-September. These committees are also involved in structuring the budget resolution, having submitted their views and estimates to the budget committees earlier in the year.

Because of the targets set by the Omnibus Budget Reconciliation Act of 1993 for discretionary categories, the authorizing and appropriating committees already know the ceilings in the respective categories for the next 5 years. Competition for discretionary dollars within the areas of domestic, defense, and international aid will be greater than ever.

Conflict will inevitably ensue. For example, with the budget authority for discretionary program dollars (see Table 1) projected from $519,000 billion for FY 1995 to $528,598 billion for FY 1998, lobbying groups will vie for scarce dollars more than ever. For the general categories of discretionary spending in recent years — defense, domestic, and international aid — defense has been slightly more than half. Any effort to increase funding above the 1993 budget settlement for natural resources programs, for example, would force reduction in another area of discretionary spending in order to preserve the overall discretionary funding target.

Conflict between the authorizing and appropriating committees may also arise. To be funded, a program must be authorized, but this action does not guarantee funding. The appropriations committees may refuse or be unable to fund a program authorized by Congress in order to preserve targets set in a discretionary area for the upcoming fiscal year.

During the spring, agency officials appear before the House and Senate appropriations subcommittees to defend their budget requests and to offer plans for the department's future goals. Usually, the full Committee on Appropriations accepts the recommendations of its subcommittees.

By May 15, the House Appropriations Committee may report the annual appropriations bills. The 1990 amendments to the 1974 budget timetable call for Congress to pass all appro-

TABLE 1 CBO Estimates of Discretionary Spending Limits for Fiscal Years 1995 Through 1998 (in millions of dollars)

Category	1995	1996	1997	1998
General-purpose spending limits as of January 23, 1995	517,067	512,891	521,234	523,098
Violent crime reduction trust fund spending limits	2,423	4,287	5,000	5,500
Total discretionary spending limits	519,490	517,178	526,234	528,598

Source: Congressional Budget Office.

priations bills by June 30, leaving the remainder of the summer for conference committees to resolve differences. If OMB finds that the appropriations for defense, for example, exceed the targets for a fiscal year, a sequester may occur within 15 days following passage of the legislation. Final passage of a budget should take place by October 1, the start of the new fiscal year. Final sequestration by OMB may take place within 15 days following the adjournment of Congress in the fall if the agreed-to targets have been exceeded.

THE REALITIES OF THE BUDGET PROCESS ON CAPITOL HILL

Unable to complete its budget work in a timely fashion, Congress funded the government on continuing resolutions for most of the 1980s. One notable exception occurred in the wake of the 1987 stock market crash, when the 100th Congress passed a budget for FY 1989 before the new fiscal year began.

Not much deficit reduction occurred during the Bush Administration. The passage of the Omnibus Budget Reconciliation Act in August 1993, at the beginning of Bill Clinton's presidency, has reduced the deficit to around $250 billion from its high of $290 billion in 1992. Even with the caps on the discretionary dollars between 1994 and 1998, set in law by the Omnibus Budget Reconciliation Act of 1993, deficits continue because many federal programs are still in place and entitlement programs have not been capped or cut.

SUMMARY

The continuing struggle over the budget reflects a lack of national consensus on the federal government's spending priorities. Conflicts arise due to the check-and-balance nature of the government, especially concerning who wields power over the national purse—Capitol Hill or the White House.

With the Republicans in control of Capitol Hill for the 104th Congress, the next 2 years, the legislative branch may more aggressively exercise its power of the purse. Believing that they have a mandate from the American people to cut the federal government, the Republicans in both the House and Senate may pass legislation that the Democratic Clinton White House may find to be unacceptable. Consensus and compromise are at the heart of the democratic form of government; they will be needed by the politicians at both ends of Pennsylvania Avenue over the next 2 years.

CHAPTER 8
Lobbying on Capitol Hill

Most Americans outside of Washington believe that a lobbyist's main work in life is to influence members of Congress with money, fancy parties, and expensive trips. Very few people realize that lobbying, or influencing legislation, is very much tied to the First Amendment of the Constitution, the right to free speech.

As a result, there is little regulation of lobbying activities. Congress did pass a law in 1946 requiring lobbyists to register with the clerk of the House and the secretary of the Senate and to report the money spent on lobbying activities on a quarterly basis. However, a Supreme Court ruling in 1954 weakened the law, and any efforts toward further regulation or reform have gone nowhere for fear of obstructing citizens' access to their elected officials.

James Madison and the other founding fathers who wrote the Constitution just over 200 years ago would not be surprised by the presence of the thousands of lobbyists in the nation's capital. The system of government they designed allows conflicting perspectives to be aired. In fact, Madison wrote, "Liberty is to faction [group] what air is to fire." It was believed that the presence of competing factions would be healthy for the Republic.

The term "lobbyist" came into common parlance in Washington by the 1830s. Depicted by political cartoonists as sinister, cigar-smoking, money-grubbing individuals, lobbyists were not highly regarded. Prestigious individuals in the 1830s, such as Daniel Webster, and many of the senators in the Gilded Age of the 1870s and 1880s often voted in favor of the interests of the bankers and the magnates of the steel, oil, and railroad industries.

What must be kept in mind, however, is that the United States has a government that responds to the presence and pressure of interest groups. Whether abolitionists in the nineteenth century who opposed slavery, anti-saloon leaguers who led the drive for prohibition in the early twentieth century, or anti-Vietnam war protestors and environmentalists of the 1960s and 1970s, all of these "special interest" groups were able to petition Congress for their causes because of our form of government.

Anywhere from 10,000 to 20,000 people lobby in Washington. Most of them believe that their purpose is to inform and to educate the members of Congress, their staffs, and the bureaucrats in the executive branch agencies in an effort to influence policy-making. The presentation of information cannot be stressed enough. If inaccurate or false information is given out, making a representative or a senator look foolish in public, all access to the member's office is usually ended and the organization's credibility is tainted.

Lobbyists represent businesses (e.g., Chamber of Commerce), state and local government (e.g., National Governors' Association), corporations (e.g., General Motors and IBM), and foreign governments and businesses (e.g., Charls E. Walker Associates, Inc.). Statistics have shown that 65 percent of Americans belong to at least one group, ranging from church-affiliated organizations to labor unions to service clubs to nationality organizations. Alexis de Tocqueville observed this "groupiness" in the country as long ago as 1825 when he wrote that Americans of all "conditions, minds, and ages, daily acquire a general taste for association and grow accustomed to the use of it." More than 5,000 organizations, or groups, are represented in Washington today.

Obviously, some of these groups are more powerful than others. But this is not to suggest that the smaller, less-monied organizations are unable to unite against the "big boys." Building coalitions of interest groups to either promote or defeat legislation has become one of the most effective lobbying techniques in recent years. Much of this kind of work takes place off Capitol Hill in offices around town. The issues are defined and strategies mapped out among the various organizations involved, although allies on one issue may well be opponents on another. Environmental legislation in recent years has seen a coalition of big industry and labor united against environmentalists and health groups. Broad-based coalitions also make the task of lobbying easier on Capitol Hill where a growing number of committees in the past 15 years has greatly increased the burden of the lobbyist.

Direct access to a representative or a senator is desired by many, but most contact on the Hill occurs between the lobbyist and congressional staff. Knowing the interests of a member's personal staff and how the office works as well as the profile of the state or district enhance an organization's ability "to get through the door."

Having obtained access, the association, corporation, or foreign government is now in the position to argue its case for or against legislation by presenting succinct and accurate information. Lobbying groups are often viewed as the issue experts in their areas. Often they are more knowledgeable about the technicalities of the legislation than the elected officials, their staffs, or a federal agency. Indeed, supported by their own staffs of lawyers and legislative experts, interest groups are frequently called on to testify before committees, to help write legislation, and to draft amendments in committee markup sessions. The more knowledgeable an organization and the greater its reputation, the more likely its input will be requested at hearings.

Prior to the early 1970s, committee hearings, markup sessions, and conference committees were not open. For the most part, all of these sessions are open today, thus allowing for greater input in more places.

In recent years, allegiance to and appreciation of the power of the elected official's constituency have grown. Being that members of Congress are sensitive to local feelings, grass-roots lobbying has increased. The ability to generate letters on an issue, to organize timely and effective local visits to a hospital or a weapons factory, and to encourage newspapers across the district or state to write editorials is a skill developed by lobbying groups based in Washington.

Modern communications and high tech have had a tremendous impact on the political process; computers can help generate mass mailings of postcards to all offices on Capitol Hill. Since 1980, mass-mailing techniques have been used by lobbyists to affect legislation. Although the high-tech generated mail still does not have the effect on elected officials that personal letters from constituents have, thousands of postcards sent on a single issue reflect some kind of interest back home.

Lobbying groups also generate grass-roots support or opposition to a particular issue through radio, television, magazines, and newspapers. Often full-page ads are run by interest groups in major newspapers, a favorite being *The Washington Post* to which just about all of the 535 members of Congress subscribe.

A final, very important lobbying technique is that of campaign support. Running for Congress has become an expensive process: the average House race costs $300,000, a Senate race over $1 million. Increasingly incumbents and challengers are accepting money from the political action committees (PACs) of interest groups.

By contributing to a candidate's campaign, it is hoped that easier access to the official would be possible and that support for the group's cause would be obtained. Such a system favors the incumbent who already has name recognition and who the organization wants to keep in office if he or she supports its position.

PACs are legal and have been around in other forms for some years. They have been subject to much criticism and have generated the fear that elected officials will become more loyal to the interests contributing to their campaign than to the interests of the district or state. Voter disinterest in the political process has contributed to this fear.

CHAPTER 9
Getting Around on Capitol Hill

Knowledge and understanding of the legislative process are crucial to gain an insight into Congress. It is often recommended that proceedings be observed and meetings held with staff and elected officials on Capitol Hill.

This chapter covers the physical layout of "the Hill," useful information regarding Hill security, and entrances to buildings for visitors, especially those who are physically disabled. It also contains suggestions for attendance at committee hearings and House and Senate floor proceedings, and an explanation of bell codes for House and Senate floor activity.

TRANSPORTATION TO CAPITOL HILL

Although Congress is one of the most open legislative bodies in the world, there is limited parking for the public. Meters are scarce and towing is strictly enforced. Public garages are a long walk from offices, and are expensive. Those who go to the Hill on a regular basis use either taxis or Washington's subway system, called the Metro. For most visitors, the Metro is the best means of transportation.

Metro Subway System

Dark-brown pylons with a large white "M" indicate the Metro station entrances. The two stations closest to Capitol Hill are the Capitol South Station (Blue and Orange Lines) on the House side of the Hill and Union Station (Red Line) on the Senate side.

Fares for Metro differ according to distances traveled and time of day (i.e., rush-hour fares cost more than nonrush-hour fares). Fares can be determined easily by consulting the route and fare maps posted at all Metro stations.

Washington's subway system is perhaps the most convenient, relatively hassle-free mode of traveling about the city and is highly recommended. Trains operate 5:30 a.m. to midnight during the week, 8 a.m. to midnight on the weekend. The schedule differs on holidays. To obtain schedule information call 637-7000, 6 a.m. to 11:30 p.m.

HOUSE AND SENATE OFFICE BUILDINGS
House Office Buildings

The map on p. 111 gives an aerial view of the layout of Capitol Hill. The office buildings of the House of Representatives are found along Independence Avenue. In descending order from that closest to the Capitol South Metro Station are the Cannon, Longworth, and Rayburn House Office Buildings. The offices of the 440 members of the House of Representatives and their staffs are housed in these buildings. House committees and their staffs also have offices there as well as in the House side of the Capitol. The map shows the O'Neill and Ford House Office Buildings, which also contain staff offices. Street addresses and room numbering systems follow:

- CHOB—Cannon House Office Building
  Independence Ave. and 1st St., S.E. (Room numbers have three digits; first digit is the floor number)
- LHOB—Longworth House Office Building
  Independence Ave. and New Jersey Ave., S.E. (Room numbers have four digits; second digit is the floor number)
- RHOB—Rayburn House Office Building
  Independence Ave. between 1st St., S.W., and South Capitol St., S.W. (Room numbers have four digits, second digit is the floor number)

Map of Capitol Hill

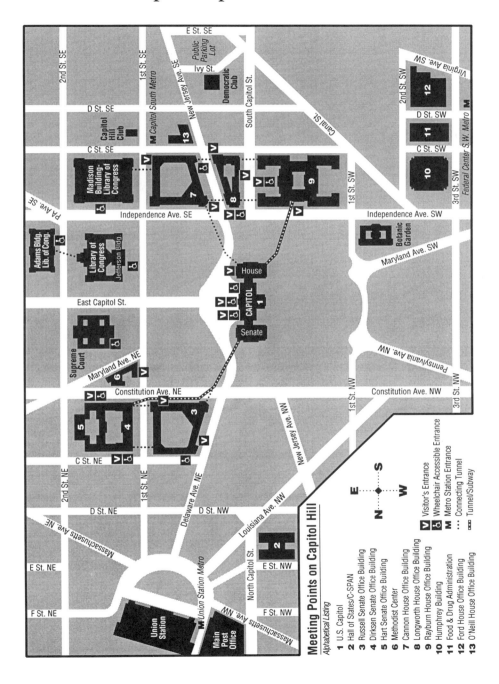

- O'NEILL HOB (formerly Annex I)
  300 New Jersey Ave., S.E.
- FORD HOB (formerly Annex II)
  2nd and D Streets, S.E.

Senate Office Buildings

The Senate office buildings are located along Constitution Avenue. These buildings also contain the senators' and their staffs' offices as well as Senate committee offices. Several Senate committee offices are also located in the Senate side of the Capitol. The street addresses and room numbering systems of the Senate office buildings follow:

- HSOB—Hart Senate Office Building
  Constitution Ave. and 2nd St., N.E. (Room numbers have three digits; first digit is the floor number)
- DSOB—Dirksen Senate Office Building
  Constitution Ave. and 1st St., N.E. (Room numbers have three digits; the first digit is the floor number)
- RSOB—Russell Senate Office Building
  Constitution Ave. and Delaware Ave., N.E. (Room numbers have three digits; the first digit is the floor number)

VISITORS' ACCESS AND SECURITY
Security

Before the era of terrorism in the 1980s, access to the Capitol and office buildings was fairly easy. However, greater threat to security has meant that visitors can enter buildings only through designated entrances. The map on p. 111 indicates visitors' entrances. Quite similar to airport security, the Capitol police — located at these designated places — inspect packages, bags, and purses before each person passes through a metal detector.

Visitors' Access

Once inside the building, the visitor is free to visit member and staff offices, attend open committee sessions, or watch the House and Senate floor proceedings if gallery passes have been obtained. (See p. 116 for information on gallery passes.) In periods of inclement weather or for access to other buildings, visitors can use a series of tunnels that connect the House and Senate office buildings and a separate subway tunnel that runs, on the House side, from the Rayburn Building to the Capitol and from each of the three Senate office buildings to the Capitol. Once in the Capitol, to continue to the Senate or House side, one must go to the first floor of the Capitol, cross the building, take the elevators to the B-level to connect with subway cars for either the House or Senate destination. The Capitol police will assist anyone in need of direction.

ACCESS FOR THE PHYSICALLY DISABLED

All street intersections on Capitol Hill have low, ramp-like curbs and all buildings have facilities to accommodate the physically disabled. Building guards know the location of these facilities, which include ramps, special elevators, telephones, and restrooms.

The map on p. 111 indicates those entrances where access ramps or other arrangements have been constructed to accommodate the needs of people using wheelchairs.

Access to the U.S. Capitol

To enter or leave the U.S. Capitol building, there are three choices. The first route is under the center stairway, on the east side of the building; the other two are at either end of the building. The ramps at either end appear to pose a problem because they lead to revolving doors. However, the doors can swing to the sides.

People who use wheelchairs can access any of the Capitol elevators. The guards at each entrance will direct them to the elevator closest to their destinations.

Subway and Tunnels to the Senate Office Buildings

Capitol guards give directions to the elevators that go to the subway and tunnels leading to the Senate office buildings. Riding the subway may prove difficult to those confined to wheelchairs. However, the tunnels are easy to traverse and lead to each of the three Senate buildings.

Subway and Tunnels to the House Office Buildings

The subway to the House side of the Hill runs only to the Rayburn Building. Like its counterpart on the Senate side, the subway from the Capitol may be difficult to board if you are confined to a wheelchair. However, as is the case on the Senate side, each of the House office buildings is accessible by tunnel from the Capitol. A Capitol guard will know where the elevators are on the House side of the Capitol to go to the tunnel that leads to the Rayburn, Longworth, or Cannon Office Buildings. In addition, there is a ramp at the B-level.

Senate Office Buildings
Hart Building

The Hart Building may be accessed by using the ramp at the front of the building on Constitution Avenue. There is no ramp on the C Street, N.E., side of the building. Corridors, doors, and elevators have been constructed to accommodate wheelchairs. All restrooms are accessible. The Hart Building and the Dirksen Building are contiguous on each floor, so that those in wheelchairs can pass conveniently from one floor to the other.

Dirksen Building

On the ground level, access to Dirksen is on the C Street, N.E., side of the building. Elevators are small but will accommodate wheelchairs. Restrooms on the first and fourth floors are accessible.

Russell Building

A ramp is located on the Delaware Avenue side of the building. Some restrooms are equipped for the physically disabled. Ask the guards for their locations.

House Office Buildings
Rayburn Building

The "horseshoe entrance" on South Capitol Street has an access ramp from the driveway promenade in front of the doors to the building. It is also possible to gain access to the building from the garage; several entrances to the building from the garage have ramps.

To get to the tunnel to the Capitol, take the elevators on the east side of the building to the G3-level. To get to the tunnel leading to the Longworth and Cannon Buildings, take the elevator to the SB-level and look for signs leading to the tunnel.

Longworth Building

The Longworth Building has first-floor access at Independence Avenue. The tunnel to the Cannon Building is on the B-level.

The Cannon Building

This building has a ramp at the New Jersey Avenue entrance. The revolving doors can be pushed to one side to allow for wheelchair access. There is a garage entrance that can be used if necessary.

ATTENDANCE AT CONGRESSIONAL COMMITTEE HEARINGS

Congressional committee hearings take place in the House and Senate offices buildings as well as in the U.S. Capitol. "Today in Congress" is a column that appears daily in *The Washington Post* when Congress is in session. It provides a listing of the day's committee hearings, their location, and the time the House and Senate will convene. Unless indicated to the contrary, hearings are open to the public and require no pass for entry.

When Congress is in session, most committee hearings take place on Tuesday, Wednesday, and Thursday.

ATTENDANCE AT THE HOUSE AND SENATE GALLERIES

A visitor must obtain gallery passes to observe floor proceedings in the House and Senate. (See pp. 119–120 for a layout of each of these chambers.) These passes may be obtained from the visitor's representative and senators' offices. Foreign visitors to Capitol Hill may obtain their passes from the Senate Sergeant-at-Arms Office in Room S-321 in the U.S. Capitol and on the House side of the Capitol by following the visitor gallery signs on the third floor to the pass desk.

HOUSE AND SENATE FLOOR ACTION

For representatives and senators to keep up to the minute on floor activity when the House and Senate are in session, a series of lights and bells can be seen and heard in all of the office buildings and the Capitol to alert the elected officials to specific activities. Explanations of their meaning are presented below.

Legislative Bells and Signals
U.S. Senate

One long ring at hour of convening. One red light remains lit while the Senate is in session. Where lights exist, they will correspond with the following rings:

1 ring: Yeas and nays.
2 rings: Quorum call.
3 rings: Call of absentees.
4 rings: Adjournment or recess.
5 rings: Seven and a half minutes remaining on yea and nay vote.
6 rings: Morning business concluded.

U.S. House of Representatives

The House rules are more complicated:

1 ring and light: Tellers (not a recorded vote).
1 long ring and light (pause) followed by 3 rings and lights: Signals the start or continuation of a notice of a quorum call.
1 long ring and light: Termination of a notice of a quorum call.
2 rings and lights: Electronically recorded vote.
2 rings and lights (pause) followed by 2 rings and lights: Manual roll call vote and the rings will be sounded again when the clerk reaches the R's.
2 rings and lights (pause) followed by 5 bells: First vote under suspension of the rules or on clustered votes (2 rings will be rung 5 minutes later). The first vote will take 15 minutes with successive votes at intervals of not less than 5 minutes. Each successive vote will be signaled by 5 rings.
3 rings and lights: Quorum call, either initially or after a notice of quorum has been converted to a regular quorum. The rings are repeated 5 minutes after the first ring.
3 rings and lights (pause) followed by 3 rings and lights: Manual quorum call. The rings will be sounded again when the clerk reaches the R's.
3 rings and lights (pause) followed by 5 rings: Quorum call in the committee of the whole, which may be followed by a 5-minute recorded vote.

4 rings and lights: Adjournment of the House.
5 rings and lights: Five-minute electronically recorded vote.
6 rings and lights: Recess of the House.

House Chamber

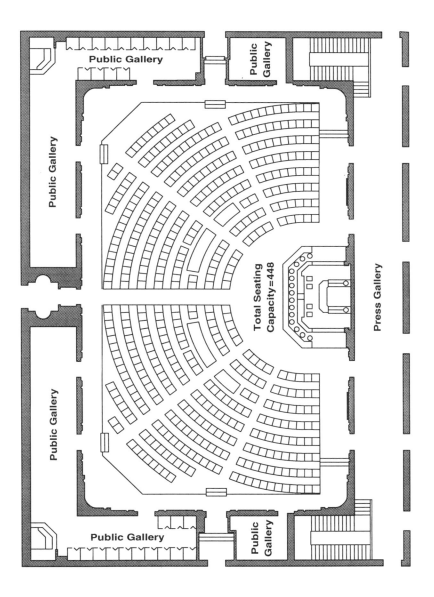

Senate Chamber

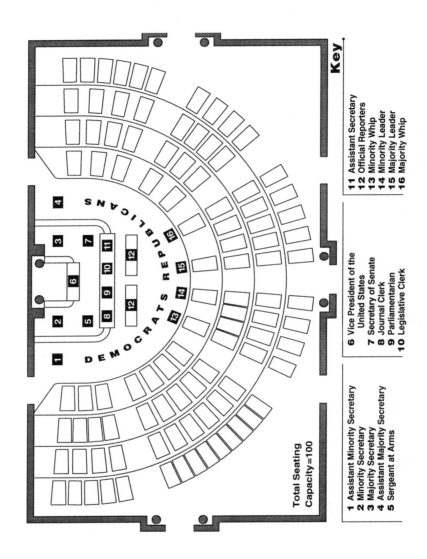

APPENDIX A
Congressional Budget Process Timetable

January	Congress convenes
Five days before the President's budget submission	Congressional Budget Office (CBO) submits sequestration preview report
Early February	Congress receives President's budget submission; Office of Management and Budget (OMB) submits sequestration preview report
Within 6 weeks after President's budget submission	Committees submit views and estimates to House Budget Committee
April 15	Congress completes action on fiscal year budget resolution
April 30	CBO and Treasury Department report on financial soundness of government-sponsored enterprises
May 15	A year's annual appropriations may be considered in the House in absence of a budget resolution
June 10	House Appropriations Committee reports last annual appropriations bill

June 30	House completes action on annual appropriations bills
Prior to July 1	The President must order a sequester within 15 days of enactment of appropriations that exceed a fiscal year's caps; if appropriations are enacted after July 1 that exceed that year's caps, the caps for the next fiscal year are lowered
July 15	President submits mid-session budget review to Congress
August 10	Presidential notification regarding exempting military personnel from sequestration
August 15	CBO submits the sequestration update report
August 20	OMB submits the sequestration update report
No later than September 15	Committees of jurisdiction in the House shall report legislation to the House to ensure the financial soundness of government-sponsored enterprises
October 1	Fiscal year begins
October 4	Target adjournment date

APPENDIX B

COMMITTEES IN THE U.S. CONGRESS

SENATE

COMMITTEE ON AGRICULTURE, NUTRITION, AND FORESTRY
Ph. 224-6901 D)　　　　　　　　Ph. 224-2035 ((R)

This committee has jurisdiction over legislation in areas such as agriculture economics and research; production, marketing, and price supports; crop insurance and farm security; food stamps; forestry and wilderness not in the public domain; inspection of meat and livestock; international food programs; and rural development and electrification. Its subcommittees include

Production and Price Competitiveness
Marketing, Inspection, and Product Promotion
Forestry, Conservation, and Rural Revitalization
Research, Nutrition, and General Legislation

COMMITTEE ON APPROPRIATIONS
Ph. 224-7200 (D)　　　　　　　　Ph. 224-3471 (R)

This committee has jurisdiction over legislation related to revenue appropriated for the support of the U.S. government; rescission of appropriated funds; and the new spending authority described in the Congressional Budget Act of 1974 as part of the budget process. Its subcommittees include

Agriculture, Rural Development, and Related Agencies
Commerce, Justice, State, and Judiciary
Defense
District of Columbia

Energy and Water Development
Foreign Operations
Interior and Related Agencies
Labor, Health and Human Services, and Education
Legislative Branch
Military Construction
Transportation and Related Agencies
Treasury, Postal Service, and General Government
Veterans Affairs, HUD, and Independent Agencies

COMMITTEE ON ARMED SERVICES
Ph. 224-3871

This committee has jurisdiction over legislation in areas such as aeronautical and space activities related to weapons systems or military operations; the common defense; the Departments of Defense, Army, Navy, and Air Force; the Strategic Defense Initiative; national security aspects of nuclear energy; and Naval petroleum reserves (not Alaska). Its subcommittees include

Airland Forces
Acquisition and Technology
Personnel
Readiness
Seapower
Strategic Forces

COMMITTEE ON BANKING, HOUSING, AND URBAN AFFAIRS
Ph. 224-7391

This committee has jurisdiction over legislation in areas such as banks and financial institutions; control of price commodities; rents and services; deposit insurance; export and foreign trade promotion; federal monetary policy; nursing home construction; public and private housing; and urban development and mass transit. Its subcommittees include

Financial Institutions and Regulatory Relief
HUD Oversight and Structure
International Finance
Securities
Housing Opportunity and Community Development

COMMITTEE ON THE BUDGET
Ph. 224-0642
This committee drafts the concurrent budget resolution in accordance with the Balanced Budget and Emergency Deficit Control Act of 1985. It also makes studies on the effect of budget outlays of relevant existing and proposed legislation, and it requests and evaluates continuing studies of tax expenditures, policies, and programs.
This committee has no subcommittees.

COMMITTEE ON COMMERCE, SCIENCE, AND TRANSPORTATION
Ph. 224-5115 (D)   *Ph. 224-1251 (R)*
This committee has jurisdiction over legislation in areas such as the Coast Guard; coastal zone management; communications; highway safety; marine fisheries and merchant marine; nonmilitary space sciences; regulation of consumer products (including testing of toxic substances); sports; and transportation. Its subcommittees include

Aviation
Communications
Consumer Affairs, Foreign Commerce, and Tourism
Oceans and Fisheries
Science, Technology, and Space
Surface Transportation and Merchant Marine

COMMITTEE ON ENERGY AND NATURAL RESOURCES
Ph. 224-4103 (D)   *Ph. 224-4971 (R)*
This committee has jurisdiction over legislation in areas such

as coal production; energy policy and regulation; extraction of minerals from areas and outer continental shelf lands; hydroelectric power; national parks; recreation and wilderness areas; oil and gas production and distribution; public lands and forests; and solar energy. Its subcommittees include

Energy Production and Regulation
Energy Research and Development
Forests and Public Land Management
Parks, Historic Preservation, and Recreation

COMMITTEE ON ENVIRONMENT AND PUBLIC WORKS
Ph. 224-8832 (D)   Ph. 224-6176 (R)

This committee has jurisdiction over legislation in areas such as air pollution; construction and maintenance of highways; environmental effects of toxic substances (not pesticides); fisheries and wildlife; ocean dumping; public works, bridges, and dams; solid waste disposal; and water pollution. Its subcommittees include

Clean Air, Wetlands, Private Property, and Nuclear Safety
Drinking Water, Fisheries, and Wildlife
Transportation and Infrastructure
Superfund, Waste Control, and Risk Assessment

COMMITTEE ON FINANCE
Ph. 224-5315 (D)   Ph. 224-4515 (R)

This committee has jurisdiction over legislation in areas such as the bonded debt of the U.S. government; customs and ports of entry; deposit of public monies; health programs under the Social Security Act; reciprocal trade agreements; and revenue measures generally. Its subcommittees include

International Trade
Long-Term Growth, Debt, and Deficit Reduction
Medicaid and Health Care for Low-Income Families
Medicare, Long-Term Care, and Health Insurance
Social Security and Family Policy

Taxation and IRS Oversight

COMMITTEE ON FOREIGN RELATIONS
Ph. 224-3953 (D) *Ph. 224-3941 (R)*
This committee has jurisdiction over legislation in areas such as land and buildings for U.S. embassies in foreign countries; boundaries of the United States; diplomatic service; foreign economic, military, and humanitarian assistance; International Monetary Fund; foreign loans; national security; treaties; and declarations of war. Its subcommittees include

African Affairs
East Asian and Pacific Affairs
European Affairs
International Economic Policy, Export, and Trade Promotion
International Operations
Near Eastern and South Asian Affairs
Western Hemisphere and Peace Corps Affairs

COMMITTEE ON GOVERNMENTAL AFFAIRS
Ph. 224-2627 (D) *Ph. 224-4751 (R)*
This committee has jurisdiction over legislation in areas such as the National Archives; census and collection of statistics; congressional organizations such as the General Accounting Office, the Congressional Research Service, and the Office of Technology Assessment; District of Columbia; intergovernmental relations; nuclear export policy; and postal service. Its subcommittees include

Oversight of Government Management and the District of Columbia
Permanent Investigations
Post Office and Civil Service

COMMITTEE ON INDIAN AFFAIRS
Ph. 224-2251
This committee studies any and all matters pertaining to the

problems and opportunities of Indians including, but not limited to, Indian land management and trust responsibilities, Indian education, health, special services, and loan programs, and Indian claims against the United States. It reports to the Senate, by bill or otherwise, its recommendations concerning matters referred to it or otherwise within its jurisdiction.

This committee has no subcommittees.

COMMITTEE ON THE JUDICIARY
Ph. 224-7703 (D) *Ph. 224-5225 (R)*

This committee has jurisdiction over legislation in areas such as apportionment of representatives; bankruptcy, mutiny, espionage, and counterfeiting; civil liberties; constitutional amendments; federal courts and judges; judicial proceedings, civil and criminal; immigration and naturalization; patents, copy rights, and trademarks; protection of trade against monopolies; and state and territorial boundary lines. Its subcommittees include

Antitrust, Business Rights, and Competition
Immigration
Administrative Oversight and the Courts
Terrorism, Technology, and Government Information
Constitution, Federalism, and Property Rights
Youth Violence

COMMITTEE ON LABOR AND HUMAN RESOURCES
Ph. 224-7675 (D) *Ph. 224-5375 (R)*

This committee has jurisdiction over legislation in areas such as education, labor, health, and public welfare; aging; agricultural colleges; arts and humanities; biomedical research and development; child labor; convict labor; equal employment opportunity; Gallaudet College, Howard University, and St. Elizabeth's Hospital; the handicapped; labor standards; private pension plans; public health; student loans; and wages and hours of labor. Its subcommittees include

Aging
Children and Families
Disability Policy
Education, Arts, and Humanities

COMMITTEE ON RULES AND ADMINISTRATION
Ph. 224-5648 (D)   *Ph. 224-6352 (R)*

This committee has jurisdiction over legislation in areas such as the administration of Senate office buildings and the Senate wing of the U.S. Capitol; Senate rules and regulations; corrupt practices; credentials and qualifications of members of the Senate; federal elections, including the election of the President, vice president, and members of the Congress; the Government Printing Office; presidential succession; and public buildings such as the Library of Congress, the Smithsonian Institution, and the Botanic Garden.

This committee has no subcommittees.

COMMITTEE ON SMALL BUSINESS
Ph. 224-5175

This committee has jurisdiction over legislation in areas such as the administration of the Small Business Administration; and the problems and regulation of American small business enterprise.

This committee has no subcommittees.

COMMITTEE ON VETERANS' AFFAIRS
Ph. 224-2074 (D)   *Ph. 224-9126 (R)*

This committee has jurisdiction over legislation in areas such as compensation of veterans; life insurance by the government on service in the Armed Forces; national cemeteries; pensions of all wars of the United States; and soldiers' and sailors' civil relief.

This committee has no subcommittees.

SELECT COMMITTEE ON ETHICS
Ph. 224-2981

This committee administers, interprets, and enforces the Senate's Code of Official Conduct; receives complaints and investigates allegations of improper conduct; recommends disciplinary action; and recommends new rules or regulations. It receives complaints about violations of Senate mail franking privileges, issues decisions, and takes other appropriate actions to enforce franking rules. The committee also investigates allegations of unauthorized disclosure of information from the Select Committee on Intelligence.

This committee has no subcommittees.

SELECT COMMITTEE ON INTELLIGENCE
Ph. 224-1700

This committee oversees and studies the intelligence activities and programs of the U.S. government. It submits appropriate proposals for legislation and makes reports to the Senate concerning intelligence activities and programs. It also assures that relevant departments and agencies provide the intelligence necessary for executive and legislative branches to make sound decisions concerning security and other vital national interests. The committee acts to ensure that intelligence activities conform with the Constitution and laws of the United States.

This committee has no subcommittees.

SPECIAL COMMITTEE ON AGING
Ph. 224-5364

This committee studies any and all matters pertaining to the problems and opportunities of older people, including, but not limited to, health maintenance, adequate income, employment, productive and rewarding activity, proper housing, and, when necessary, access to care or assistance. No proposed legislation is referred to the committee, and the committee cannot report by bill, or otherwise have legislative jurisdiction. It reports to the Senate, not less than once each year, the results of its studies and its recommendations.

This committee has no subcommittees.

U.S. HOUSE OF REPRESENTATIVES

COMMITTEE ON AGRICULTURE
Ph. 225-1867 (D)   *Ph. 225-2171 (R)*

This committee has jurisdiction over legislation in areas such as adulteration of seeds and protection of birds and animals in forest reserves; agriculture generally; agricultural colleges and experiment stations; agricultural production, marketing, and prices; crop insurance; dairy industry; forestry in general and forest reserves other than those created from the public domain; meat and livestock inspection; rural development; human nutrition; and food inspection. Its subcommittees include

Department Operations, Nutrition, and Foreign Agriculture
General Farm Commodities
Livestock, Dairy, and Poultry
Resource Conservation, Research, and Forestry
Risk Management and Specialty Crops

COMMITTEE ON APPROPRIATIONS
Ph. 225-3481 (D)   *Ph. 225-2771 (R)*

This committee has jurisdiction over legislation related to revenue appropriated for the support of the U.S. government; rescission of appropriated funds; and the new spending authority described in the Congressional Budget Act of 1974 as part of the budget process. Its subcommittees include

Agriculture, Rural Develpment, FDA, and Related Agencies
Commerce, Justice, State, and Judiciary

District of Columbia
Energy and Water Development
Foreign Operations, Export Financing, and Related Programs
Interior
Labor, Health and Human Services, and Education
Legislative Branch
Military Construction
National Security
Transportation
Treasury, Postal Service, and General Government
VA, HUD, and Independent Agencies

COMMITTEE ON BANKING AND FINANCIAL SERVICES
Ph. 225-4247 (D)   Ph. 225-7502 (R)

This committee has jurisdiction over legislation in areas such as banks and banking, including deposit insurance, federal monetary policy and has primary jurisdiction over the Glass-Steagall Act, which governs security activities of banks; money and credit, including currency and notes; urban development; private and public housing; international finance; and international financial and monetary organizations. Its subcommittees include

Capital Markets, Securities and Government-Sponsored Enterprises
Domestic and International Monetary Policy
Financial Institutions and Consumer Credit
General Oversight and Investigations
Housing and Community Opportunity

COMMITTEE ON THE BUDGET
Ph. 226-7200 (D)   Ph. 226-7270 (R)

This committee drafts the concurrent budget resolution in accordance with the Balanced Budget and Emergency Deficit Control Act of 1985. It also makes studies on the effect of budget outlays of relevant, existing, and proposed legislation, and it requests and evaluates continuing studies of tax expenditures, policies, and programs.

This committee has no subcommittees.

COMMITTEE ON COMMERCE

Ph. 225-3641 (D)   *Ph. 225-2927 (R)*

This committee has jurisdiction over legislation in areas such as interstate and foreign commerce generally; national energy policy and energy information; measures relating to the exploration, production, storage, supply, marketing, pricing, and regulation of all fossil fuels and solar energy; conservation of energy resources; interstate energy compacts; and travel and tourism. Its subcommittees include

Commerce, Trade, and Hazardous Materials
Energy and Power
Health and the Environment
Oversight and Investigations
Telecommunications and Finance

COMMITTEE ON ECONOMIC AND EDUCATIONAL OPPORTUNITIES

Ph. 225-3725 (D)   *Ph. 225-4527 (R)*

This committee has jurisdiction over legislation in areas such as measures relating to education and labor generally; child labor; convict labor; labor standards and statistics; mediation and arbitration of labor disputes; food programs for school children; vocational rehabilitation; wages and hours of labor; and welfare of minors. Its subcommittees include

Early Childhood, Youth, and Families
Employer-Employee Relations
Oversight and Investigations
Postsecondary Education, Training, and Lifelong Learning
Worker Protections

COMMITTEE ON GOVERNMENT REFORM AND OVERSIGHT

Ph. 225-5051 (D)   *Ph. 225-5074 (R)*

This committee has jurisdiction over legislation in areas such as budget and accounting measures other than budget and appropriations; reorganization of the executive branch of government; intergovernmental relations; national archives; and overall economy and efficiency of government operations and activities, including federal procurement. Its subcommittees include

Civil Service
District of Columbia
Government Management, Information, and Technology
Human Resources and Intergovernmental Affairs
National Economic Growth, Natural Resources, and Regulatory Affairs
National Security, International Affairs, and Criminal Justice
Postal Service

COMMITTEE ON HOUSE OVERSIGHT

Ph. 225-2061 (D)   *Ph. 225-8281 (R)*

This committee has jurisdiction over legislation in areas including employment of persons by the House such as clerks for committees and reporters for debates; matters relating to the Library of Congress, the Botanic Garden, and the House Library; matters relating to the printing and correction of the Congressional Record; assignment of office space for House members; House members' campaign funds; and House members' retirement.

This committee has no subcommittees.

COMMITTEE ON INTERNATIONAL RELATIONS

Ph. 225-1273 (D)   *Ph. 225-5021 (R)*

This committee has jurisdiction over legislation in areas such as relations between the United States and foreign nations gen-

Appendix B

erally; acquisition of land and buildings for embassies in foreign countries; U.S. boundaries; foreign loans; intervention abroad and declarations of war; diplomatic service; American Red Cross; United Nations' organizations; and international education. Its subcommittees include

Africa
Asia and the Pacific
International Economic Policy and Trade
International Operations and Human Rights
Western Hemisphere

COMMITTEE ON THE JUDICIARY
Ph. 225-6906 (D) *Ph. 225-3951 (R)*

This committee has jurisdiction over legislation in areas such as judicial proceedings, civil and criminal generally; apportionment of representatives; bankruptcy, mutiny, espionage, and counterfeiting; civil liberties; constitutional amendments; federal courts and judges; immigration and naturalization; suits against the United States; patent office; presidential succession; codification of the statutes of the United States; and communist and other subversive activities affecting the internal security of the United States. Its subcommittees include

Commercial and Administrative Law
Constitution
Courts and Intellectual Property
Crime
Immigration and Claims

COMMITTEE ON NATIONAL SECURITY
Ph. 225-4151

This committee has jurisdiction over legislation in areas such as the Department of Defense, generally, as well as the Army, Navy, and Air Force; the Strategic Defense Initiative; ammunition depots, forts, and arsenals; naval petroleum and oil shale preserves; pay, promotion, and retirement of armed forces members; military applications of nuclear energy; selective service; materials for the common defense; and merchant marine issues. Its subcommittees include

Military Installations and Facilities
Military Personnel
Military Procurement
Military Readiness
Military Research and Development

COMMITTEE ON RESOURCES
Ph. 225-6065 (D) *Ph. 225-2761 (R)*

This committee has jurisdiction over legislation in areas such as forest reserves and national parks created from the public domain; Geological Survey; interstate compacts for irrigation purposes; Indian affairs; the insular possessions of the United States; military parks and battlefields; mining interests generally; petroleum conservation on the public lands; regulation of domestic nuclear energy; fisheries and endangered species; and the Trans-Alaska pipeline. Its subcommittees include

Energy and Mineral Resources
Fisheries, Wildlife, and Oceans
National Parks, Forests, and Lands
Native American and Insular Affairs
Water and Power Resources

COMMITTEE ON RULES
Ph. 225-9486 (D) *Ph. 225-9191 (R)*

This committee has jurisdiction over legislation in areas such as the rules and joint rules (excluding ethics), and order of business of the House; emergency waivers (under the Budget Act of 1985) of the required reporting date for bills and resolutions authorizing new budget authority; and recesses and final adjournment. Its subcommittees include

Legislative Process
Rules and Organization of the House

COMMITTEE ON SCIENCE
Ph. 225-6375 (D)   Ph. 225-6371 (R)
This committee has jurisdiction over legislation in areas such as astronautical and energy research and development; NASA; National Science Foundation; outer space, including exploration and control thereof; scientific research and development in federally owned nonmilitary energy laboratories; civil aviation; and National Weather Service. Its subcommittees include
Basic Research
Energy and Environment
Space and Aeronautics
Technology

COMMITTEE ON SMALL BUSINESS
Ph. 225-4038 (D)   Ph. 225-5821 (R)
This committee has jurisdiction over legislation in areas such as assistance to and protection of small business, including financial aid; and participation of small-business enterprises in federal procurement and government contracts. Its subcommittees include
Government Programs
Procurement, Exports, and Business Opportunities
Regulation and Paperwork
Tax and Finance

COMMITTEE ON TRANSPORTATION AND INFRASTRUCTURE
Ph. 225-4472 (D)   Ph. 225-9446 (R)
This committee has jurisdiction over legislation in areas such as flood control and improvement of rivers and harbors; measures relating to all of the buildings on Capitol Hill as well as the Botanic Garden, the Library of Congress, and the Smithsonian;

government buildings in the District of Columbia; oil and other pollution of navigable waters; public buildings and grounds in the United States generally; water power; roads and safety thereof; railroad and inland waterways transportation; U.S. Coast Guard; and measures relating to transportation regulation agencies including the Federal Railroad Administration and Amtrak. Its subcommittees include

Aviation
Coast Guard and Maritime Transportation
Public Buildings and Economic Development
Railroads
Surface Transportation
Water Resources and Environment

COMMITTEE ON STANDARDS OF OFFICIAL CONDUCT
Ph. 225-7103

This committee has jurisdiction over legislation in areas relating to the Code of Official Conduct.

This committee has no subcommittees.

COMMITTEE ON VETERANS' AFFAIRS
Ph. 225-9756 (D)   *Ph. 225-3527 (R)*

This committee has jurisdiction over legislation in areas such as compensation of veterans; life insurance by the government on service in the Armed Forces; national cemeteries; pensions of all wars of the United States; and soldiers' and sailors' civil relief. Its subcommittees include

Compensation, Pension, Insurance, and Memorial Affairs
Education, Training, Employment, and Housing
Hospitals and Health Care

COMMITTEE ON WAYS AND MEANS
Ph. 225-4021 (D)   *Ph. 225-3625 (R)*

This committee has jurisdiction over legislation in areas such as customs, collection districts, and ports of entry; reciprocal trade agreements; revenue measures generally and to insular possessions; the bonded debt of the United States; deposit of public monies; tax exempt foundations and charitable trusts; national social security, except health care and facilities programs that are supported by payroll deductions and work incentive programs; and transportation of dutiable goods. Its subcommittees include

Health
Human Resources
Oversight
Social Security
Trade

PERMANENT SELECT COMMITTEE ON INTELLIGENCE
Ph. 225-4121

This committee has jurisdiction over the intelligence community, including the intelligence activities of the Central Intelligence Agency (CIA), Defense Intelligence Agency (DIA), National Security Agency, other agencies of DOD, and Departments of State, Justice and Treasury. Its subcommittees include

Human Intelligence, Analysis, and Counterintelligence
Technical and Tactical Intelligence

JOINT COMMITTEES

JOINT ECONOMIC COMMITTEE
Ph. 224-5171

This committee is responsible for conducting studies of issues associated with the President's Economic Report and counseling members of Congress on economic issues affecting the nation.

This committee has no subcommittees.

JOINT COMMITTEE ON THE LIBRARY
Ph. 224-3753

This committee is responsible for oversight of the Library of Congress; cultivation and maintenance of the Botanic Garden; donations made to the library. It addresses matters about the receipt and placement of statues and other artwork in and around the Capitol.

This committee has no subcommittees.

JOINT COMMITTEE ON PRINTING
Ph. 224-5241

This committee is responsible for the printing and distribution policy for federal government publications and acts to alleviate neglect, delay, duplication, or waste in public printing and distribution. It also establishes standards and specifications for paper used by the government in printing and binding operations and oversees the operation of the U.S. Government Printing Office (GPO), federal overseas printing plants, and the Federal Printing Procurement Program (i.e., printing purchased from the private sector through competitive bids). It promotes public access to federal publications, the Depository Library Program, and the GPO sales program.

This committee has no subcommittees.

JOINT COMMITTEE ON TAXATION
Ph. 225-3621

This committee is responsible for supervising the overall operation, administration, and simplification of federal tax laws and administering tax refunds in excess of $200,000. Its staff provides tax expertise for Congress and the tax-writing committees.

This committee has no subcommittees.

APPENDIX C
SUGGESTED READINGS

Baker, Ross K. 1995. *House and Senate,* 2nd ed. New York: W. W. Norton.

Birnbaum, Jeffrey H., and Alan S. Murray. 1987. *Showdown at Gucci Gulch: Lawmakers, Lobbyists, and the Unlikely Triumph of Tax Reform.* New York: Random House.

Collender, Stanley E. 1993. *The Guide to the Federal Budget.* Washington, D.C.: Urban Institute Press.

Davidson, Roger H., and Walter J. Oleszek. 1990. *Congress and Its Members,* 3rd ed. Washington, D.C.: Congressional Quarterly.

Dionne, E.J. Jr. 1992. *Why Americans Hate Politics.* New York: Simon and Schuster.

Drew, Elizabeth. 1979. *Senator.* New York: Simon and Schuster.

Ehrenhalt, Alan. 1992. *The United States of Ambition: Politicians, Power, and the Pursuit of Office.* New York: Times Books.

Fenno, Richard F., Jr. 1973. *Congressmen in Committees.* Boston: Little, Brown & Co.

Galloway, George B. 1976. *History of the House of Representatives.* Rev. ed. by Sidney Wise. New York: Thomas Y. Crowell.

Malbin, Michael J. 1979. *Unelected Representatives: Congressional Staff and the Future of Representative Government.* New York: Basic Books.

Mann, Thomas E., and Norman J. Ornstein, eds. 1981. *The New Congress.* Washington, D.C.: American Enterprise Institute for Public Policy Research.

Mayhew, David R. 1974. *Congress: The Electoral Connection*. New Haven: Yale University Press.

Oleszek, Walter J. 1988. *Congressional Procedures and the Policy Process*, 3rd ed. Washington, D.C.: Congressional Quarterly.

Redman, Eric. 1973. *The Dance of Legislation*. New York: Simon and Schuster.

Reid, T. R. 1990. *Congressional Odyssey: The Saga of a Senate Bill*. San Francisco: W. H. Freeman.

Sabato, Larry J. 1985. *PAC Power: Inside the World of Political Action Committees*. New York: W.W. Norton.

Schick, Allen. 1980. *Congress and Money*. Washington, D.C.: Urban Institute.

Schick, Allen. 1995. *The Federal Budget: Politics, Policy, Process*. Washington, D.C.: Brookings Institution.

Wayne, Stephen. 1978. *The Legislative Presidency*. New York: Harper and Row.

White, Joseph, and Aaron Wildavsky. 1989. *The Deficit and the Public Interest*. Berkeley: University of California Press.

Wildavsky, Aaron. 1988. *The New Politics of the Budgetary* Boston: Scott Foresman.

APPENDIX D
WOODS INSTITUTE SERVICE PROFILE

The Woods Institute of Washington, D.C., offers seminars for businesses and organizations that need to know about the legislative operations in the U.S. Congress as well as the state, local, and national government relations within the federal system. Speakers and course materials are chosen to meet a client's needs. Members of Congress and their staffs, elected state and local officials, journalists, and government scholars are among the speakers who participate in the institute's programs. Clients include the U.S. Forest Service, the National Park Service, U.S. Department of State, Naval Test Pilot School, Naval Air Systems Command, U.S. Information Agency, National Association of Counties, Conference of Mayors, Georgetown University, and McDonnell Douglas Corporation.

Dr. Patricia D. Woods, director of the institute, has nearly 20 years of experience working at the federal, state, and local levels. More than 10,000 executives, managers, and support staff from 50 federal agencies and private industry have participated in her courses. Prior to the establishment of the Woods Institute, she was a visiting professor with the Government Affairs Institute of the Office of Personnel Management in Washington, D.C., where she lectured on the Congress, the federal budget and the economy, legislative tracking, and federalism. Comments on her courses have included the following: "I should have had this course when I first entered the federal government," "I now have a greater awareness of the budget and legislation affecting my job," "All Americans should take this course on the Congress," "I have a better understanding of the pressures that face elected officials," and "An outstanding macro view of the Pentagon budget process."

Her expertise in state and local government comes from more than 7 years with the Louisiana Legislature in Baton Rouge and the National Association of Counties in Washington, D.C.

CURRICULUM

The institute's curriculum includes seminars on:
- The Congressional Committee Hearing Process: Testifying Before Congress
  - Congressional Operations: A Study of the U.S. Congress
  - Congress and Elections
  - The Federal Budget and the Congressional Budget Process
  - The Defense Budget Process in the Washington Community
  - The Washington Foreign Policy Process
  - Federalism: Intergovernmental Relations in the Federal System
  - Federal Government Operations
  - Selected Topics in American History and Government

Glossary of Legislative Terms

act The term for legislation that has passed both houses of Congress and has been signed by the President, or was passed over his veto, thus becoming law.

amendment A legislator's proposal to alter the language or stipulations in a bill or act.

bill The form in which legislative proposals before Congress are introduced. Bills in the House of Representatives are designated as H.R. # and Senate bills as S. #.

budget This document, sent to Congress by the President in January each year, estimates government revenues and expenditures for the following fiscal year and recommends specific appropriations.

budget deficit The amount by which government budget outlays exceed budget receipts for a given fiscal year.

clean bill When a committee makes major changes in a bill, the chairman usually incorporates them into what is left of the original bill and introduces a "clean bill" with a new number.

cloture The process of ending a filibuster in the Senate. Sixty senators must vote for cloture for it to be invoked, thereby ending the filibuster.

Committee of the Whole Working title of what is formally "The Committee of the Whole House of Representatives on the State of the Union." It has no fixed membership and comprises 100 members who participate in legislative debate on the floor of the House.

concurrent resolution A resolution that must pass both the House and the Senate, but does not require the President's signature, nor does it have the force of law. It is designated as S.Con.Res. or H.Con.Res.

conference The meeting between members of the House and Senate to reconcile the differences in their respective bills on a related measure.

Congressional Record The daily printed account of the procedures in both the House and Senate chambers.

continuing resolution A resolution enacted by Congress and signed by the President that allows federal agencies to continue operations until their regular appropriations bills are enacted.

engrossed bill The final copy of a bill that has passed the House or the Senate. The text amended by floor action is incorporated into the bill.

enrolled bill The final copy of a bill that has been passed in identical form by both the House and the Senate.

filibuster Prolonged debate by a senator or senators in the minority to delay a vote on a bill that probably would pass if brought to a vote.

germane Pertaining to the subject matter of the measure at hand.

hearings Committee session for hearing witnesses' testimony.

House Calendar A listing for action by the House of Representatives of all public bills that do not pertain to tax appropriations.

joint committee A committee composed of a specified number of representatives and senators for special policy studies.

joint resolution A resolution that must pass both the House and Senate, receive the President's signature, and has the force of law if so approved.

majority leader Chief strategist and floor leader for the party in control of either the House or the Senate.

majority whip The assistant majority leader in both the House and the Senate.

markup Refers to a process by which congressional subcommittees and committees revise a bill before reporting it to full committee or to the full House or Senate, respectively.

minority leader Floor leader for the minority party.

minority whip Chief assistant to the minority leader.

override A process whereby Congress annuls, or overrides, a presidential veto of a bill. It requires a two-thirds vote in each house of Congress.

pocket veto An action of the President in withholding his approval of a bill after Congress has adjourned either for the year or for a specified period.

president of the Senate The chief presiding officer of this chamber, also the U.S. vice president.

president pro tempore The chief officer in the Senate in the absence of the Senate president. He or she is usually the oldest member of the majority party.

public law A measure that has passed both houses of Congress and has been signed by the President. Laws are listed numerically by Congress; for example, Public Law 90-365 indicates that the bill was passed by the 90th Congress. It is often abbreviated as P.L.

recorded vote A vote upon which each member's stand is individually made known.

resolution A measure passed only by the chamber that introduced it. S.Res. or H.Res. deals with business pertaining only to one house or the other.

rider An unrelated measure attached to a congressional bill to compel the President to accept the bill with its rider. The President cannot veto part of a bill.

rule   This term has two congressional meanings. A rule, as listed in the House or Senate handbook, states how House and Senate business should be conducted. Secondly it means the procedure established by the House Rules Committee for floor debate on a bill.

sequestration   This term refers to the automatic budget-cutting mechanism called for in a given fiscal year.

supplemental appropriations   Considered after passage of regular (annual) appropriations bills. They are acted on before the end of the fiscal year to which they apply.

teller vote   Used in the House, but not in the Senate, to record the totals of yeas and nays and not how the members voted individually.

unanimous consent   Used in lieu of a vote on noncontroversial motions, amendments, or bills.

Union Calendar   A House calendar containing bills that directly or indirectly appropriate money or raise revenue.

veto   An action by the President to reject a bill passed by Congress.

views and estimates   Reports prepared by House and Senate standing committees on a President's budget request for a given fiscal year that are submitted by them to the budget committees to assist in developing the budget resolution.

INDEX

A

Adams, John, 79
Age Discrimination and
    Rehabilitation Act, 68
Administrative assistants, 69, 71
Appropriations
    supplemental, 150
    see also Standing committees
Aspin, Les, 41
Authorization, *see* Standing
    committees
Armey, Dick, 35

B

Baker, Howard, 37
Balanced budget amendment, 38
Balanced Budget and Emergency
    Deficit Control Act, 94
Biden, Joseph, 72
Bills
    amendment (markup)
        process, 4, 5, 58, 60-61,
        74, 147, 149
    clean, 49, 147
    committee action on, 2-5
    committee report on, 62
    definition, 147
    engrossed, 148
    enrolled, 148
    floor consideration of, 5-6,
        37
    legislative history, 62
    passage, 5, 11-29 (table), 45
    promotion of, 58-59, 74

riders, 149
scheduling of, 37
see also Legislation; Legislative
    process
Bingaman, Jeff, 55
Black Caucus, 44
Bonoir, David, 36
Bork, Robert, 64
Bowsher, Charles A., 76
Budget
    congressional power over, 91
    deficit reduction, 94-97, 101
    deficit spending, 91-92, 94,
        147
    definition, 147
    discretionary, appropriated
        money, 97, 99
    executive control over, 101
    and tax reform, 37, 86, 88-
        90, 94-97
    see also Standing committees
Budget and Accounting Act, 75,
    89-90
Budget and Impoundment
    Control Act, 76, 91, 92,
    93, 94
Budget Enforcement Act of 1990,
    95-100
Budget process
    authorization and
        appropriation, 91, 99-100
    congressional role, 93-98
    executive branch, 93, 95, 97
    funding by continuing
        resolution, 94, 100

phases of, 97-100
realities of, 100-101
reconciliation, 98
resolution, 98
spending ceilings and targets, 93-101
timetable, 93-94, 97, 121-122
Bureau of the Budget, 90
Bush, George, 8, 56, 81, 86, 95, 97, 100
Byrd, Robert C., 87

C

Cannon, Clarence, 46
Cannon House Office Building, 110, 115
Capitol Hill
access for physically disabled, 113-115
access for visitors, 113
bells and signals for floor action, 116-118
committee hearings, attendance at, 116
galleries at House and Senate, public attendance at, 116
House office buildings, 110
map, 111
security, 112-113
Senate office buildings, 112
transportation to, 109-110
Carter, Jimmy, 56, 80-81, 85-86, 88
Caseworkers, 69-70, 71-72
Caucuses, *see* Black Caucus; Democratic Caucus; Issue caucuses
Chairpersons, *see* Committee chairpersons
Christensen, Jon, 54
Civil Rights Act of 1964, 66, 68, 81

Clinton, Bill, 38, 63, 77, 82, 86, 97, 101
Cloture, 147
Committee chairpersons
changes in, 53
of conference committees, 6
power of, 2, 4-5, 6-7, 32, 34, 41-43, 45, 47, 49, 59-60, 81, 89
seniority system, 45-46
Committees
access to members, 74
assignment to, 31, 32, 34, 41, 42, 43, 53-56
function of, 45
hearings, 56-64; *see also* Hearings; Legislative hearings
joint, 51
majority/minority ratio, 54
membership on, 50-51, 53-56, 58-59
of party organizations, 40
political action, 7, 99-100
prestigious/powerful, 54, 56
quorum, 60-61
referral of bills to, 2, 43, 49-50, 55
rules changes affecting system of, 46
select (special), 48, 50-51
staff, 66-68, 73-74
structure of, 55-56
subcommittees, 45-46
types of, 46-52
see also Committee chairpersons; Conference committees; House committees; Senate committees; Standing committees; Study committees
Conference committees
negotiations, 7

Index

role of, 48, 51-52
selection of members, 6-7,
    51-52
size of, 52
Congress
    committees, *see* Committees;
        House committees; Senate
        committees
    information resources in, 84
    leadership and power centers
        in, 31-44
    nature of, and legislative
        process, 1-2, 34, 52
    staff, *see* Staff on Capitol Hill
    see also House of
        Representatives; Senate
Congressional Accountability Act,
    68
Congressional Budget Office
    role of, 92, 98
    staff of, 65, 67, 69, 76-77
Congressional member
    organizations, 44; *see also*
    specific organizations
Congressional Record, 148
Congressional Research Service,
    staff of, 65, 67, 75
Connelly, Tom, 46
Constitutional amendments, 60
Craig, Larry, 55
Contract with America, 34, 35,
    59, 97

D

Daschle, Thomas, 38
Debate
    informality in Senate, 35
    limits on, 5
DeLay, Tom, 36
Democratic Caucus
    committee organization of, 40
    disciplining of members, 41
    role of, 36, 39

Democratic Conference
    committee organization of, 40
    role of, 39
Democrats
    Congressional Campaign
        Committee, 42
    leadership positions on
        Capitol Hill, 31-32
    nature of, 35
    party organizations on
        Capitol Hill, 39-41
    Policy Committee, 35, 38, 42
    Senate Campaign Committee,
        40, 43
    Steering and Policy
        Committee, 32
    Steering Committee, 35, 38,
        42
Dingell, John, 5, 49
Dirksen Senate Office Building,
    112, 114
District offices, staff in, 70, 71
Dole, Elizabeth, 88
Dole, Robert, 37-38

E

Economic stimulus package, 38
Ehrlichman, John, 85
Eisenhower, Dwight, 82
Equal Employment Opportunity
    Commission, 66
Executive branch
    budget formulation, 93, 98
    domestic policy staff, 87
    influence on hearings, 59
    information resources, 84
    lobbying, 82-87
    role in legislative process, 59,
        62, 79-90
    separation of powers from
        legislative branch, 79
    see also President
Executive privilege, 85

F

F-18 fighter planes, 49
Fair Labor Standards Act, 68
Family and Medical Leave Act, 68
Family Leave bill, 86
Federal Savings and Loan Insurance Corporation, 63
Feinstein, Diane, 56
Filibustering, 5, 38, 147, 148
Foley, Thomas S., 34
Ford, Gerald, 38, 83, 85
Ford, Wendell, 39
Friedersdorf, Max, 85, 86

G

General Accounting Office
 authorization of funding for, 62
 comptroller general, 65
 function of, 75-76
 staff of, 65, 67, 69, 75-76
General Revenue Sharing, 92
Gephardt, Richard A., 35
Gingrich, Newt, 32, 34
Gorsuch, Ann Burford, 63
Government, downsizing of, 97, 101
Gramm, Phil, 39, 41
Gramm-Rudman-Hollings bill, 94-95, 96
Grand Island National Recreation Area Act, 9
Great Society Program, 81, 83, 91
Griffin, Patrick J., 87

H

Haldeman, H. R., 85
Hamilton, Lee, 55
Harlow, Bryce, 85
Hart Senate Office Building, 112, 114
Health care plan, 82
Hearings
 confirmation, 56-58, 64
 field, 58
 investigation, 56-58, 63
 oversight, 57-58, 62-63
 public attendance at, 116
 scheduling of, 58
 tone and content of, 58
 types of, 56-58
 see also Legislative hearings
Hill, Anita, 55
House committees
 Aging, 51
 Agriculture, 55, 131
 Appropriations, 42, 47, 54, 91, 92, 98-99, 132
 Armed Services, 41, 46-47, 55
 assignment to, 34, 41
 Banking and Financial Services, 132
 Banking, Housing, and Urban Affairs, 132
 Budget, 41, 92, 99, 133
 changes in membership on, 4-5, 54-55
 Commerce, 47, 54, 133
 Committee of the Whole, 147
 Democrat, 42
 District of Columbia, 46, 51
 Economics and Educational Opportunities, 133
 Energy and Commerce, 5, 47, 49, 56
 Foreign Affairs, 56
 Government Reform and Oversight, 47, 62, 134
 House Oversight, 134-135
 Indian Affairs, 51
 Intelligence, 51
 International Relations, 55, 135
 Judiciary, 56, 60, 135-136
 Merchant Marine and Fisheries, 46, 51

Index

Natural Resources, 47
National Security, 47, 49, 55, 136
number of, 47, 73
Policy, 41-42
Post Office and Civil Service, 46, 51
Republican, 34, 41-42
Resources, 47, 136
Rules, 6, 30, 34, 37, 42, 137
Science, 55, 137
select, 50-51
Small Business, 137
Standards of Official Conduct, 138
Steering, 41
Transportation and Infrastructure, 47, 138
Veterans' Affairs, 138-139
Ways and Means, 2, 42, 50, 54, 89, 139
see also Joint committees
House of Representatives
bells and signals for floor action, 117-118
calendar, 5, 148, 150
constituency size of members, 1
debate in, 5
galleries, attendance at, 116
leadership positions in, 32, 36, 40
majority leader, 31-32, 33, 34-35
majority whip, 32, 33, 35-36
minority leader, 31-32, 33, 35
minority whip, 32, 33, 35-36
office buildings, 110, 112
parliamentarian, 33, 34
party organizations, 39-41
personal staff in, 71-72
scheduling of hearings on legislation, 5-6
size of, 5
speaker, 32-34
zone whips, 33, 36

I

Interest groups
coalitions of, 105
influence of, 103-107
number of, 104
role of, 4, 104-105
see also Issue caucuses; *and* specific caucuses
Iran-Contra Affair, 41, 63
Issue caucuses, 44; *see also* specific caucuses

J

Jackson-Lee, Sheila, 55
Jefferson, Thomas, 79
Johnson, Lyndon B., 81, 83, 91
Joint committees
definition on, 148
Economic, 140
Library, 140
Printing, 140
Taxation, 141
Judicial branch, *see* Supreme Court

K

Kennedy, John F., 81, 83
Kissinger, Henry, 59

L

Latham, Tom, 55
Lavelle, Rita, 63
Legislation
committee/subcommittee jurisdiction over, 2-3
constitutionality of, 8
course of, 2-3
revenue-raising, 89; *see also* Budget, and tax reform
vetoes, 8, 149
volume of submission, 1-2, 5, 43

"whip notice" of, 36
see also Bills; Resolutions
Legislative affairs staff, 82, 87-88;
    see also White House
    Office of Congressional
    Relations
Legislative assistants, 69
Legislative hearings
    attendance, 59-61
    on constitutional
        amendments, 60
    executive branch influence
        on, 59
    full-committee, 4, 49
    purpose of, 55
    scheduling of, 4-5, 30, 58-60
    staff role during, 74
    witnesses, 59-60
Legislative process
    amendment of bills, 4-5, 49,
        58, 60-61, 74
    committee action on bills, 2-5; *see*
        also Legislative hearings
    conference stage, 6-7, 148
    floor consideration stage, 5-6,
        37, 74
    President's role, 8, 79-90
    referral to committee, 2-5,
        49-50
    Supreme Court's role in, 8
Library of Congress, Legislative
    Reference Service, 75
Lobbyists/Lobbying
    access to congressional staff,
        105
    computers and, 88, 106
    and First Amendment, 103
    grass-roots, 87, 105-106
    for hearings on bills, 58
    historical background on,
        103-104
    regulation on, 103
    role, 4, 7, 61, 88
    techniques, 105
    White House, 82-83, 85-87
    see also Interest groups
Longworth House Office
    Building, 110, 115
Lott, Trent, 39

M

MacGregor, Clark, 85
Madison, James, 103
Majority leaders
    duties of, 32, 34-35, 37, 149
    election of, 34
    House, 33, 34-35
    powers of, 33, 38
    Senate, 33, 37-38
Majority whips, duties of, 32, 35-
    36, 149
Marbury vs. Madison, 8
Markup, 4, 58, 61, 74, 149
Marshall, John, 8
Metro subway system, 109-110
Mills, Wilbur, 46
Minority leaders, duties of, 31-32,
    35, 38, 149
Minority whips, duties of, 32, 35-
    36, 149
Moore, Frank, 85
Moseley-Braun, Carol, 56
MX missiles, 41, 75

N

Nethercutt, George, 54
New Deal program, 79, 90
New Freedom program, 79
New Frontier program, 79, 83
New York State Delegation, 45
Nixon, Richard, 83, 91-92
North American Free Trade
    Agreement, 86

O

O'Brien, Lawrence, 83
Occupational Safety And Health
    Act, 68

Index

Office of Fair Employment
  Practices, 66
Office of Management and
  Budget, 76-77, 92, 93, 95,
  100
Office of Technology Assessment,
  staff of, 65, 67, 69, 76
Omnibus Budget Reconciliation
  Act, 98, 99, 101
Omnibus Trade and
  Competitiveness Act of
  1988, 2, 52
O'Neill, Tip, 34

P

Panama Canal Treaties, 86
Parliamentary government, 93
Parliamentarians, role of, 2, 34, 47
Patman, Wright, 46
Perry, William, 64
Personal staff
  administrative assistants, 69
  budget for, 71, 72
  caseworkers, 69-70, 71-72
  in district offices, 70
  executive secretary, 70
  in House and Senate, 71-72
  legislative assistants, 69
  press secretary, 69
  role of, 68-69, 71-72
  salaries of, 71
  types of, 67, 68-70
Physically disabled, access for
  House offices, 115
  Senate offices, 114-115
  subways and tunnels to office
    buildings, 114
  U.S. Capitol, 113-114
Pocket veto, 149
Political action committees, role
  of, 7, 106-107
Political parties
  disciplining of members, 39,
    41
  leadership, 31
  organizations on Capitol Hill,
    35-36, 39-43
President
  executive privilege, 85
  impoundment of funds by,
    85, 92
  growth of influence, 89
  interaction with Congress,
    79-82
  legislative successes, 82, 85,
    86, 88, 92
  role in budget and tax areas,
    88-90
  role in legislative process, 8,
    79-90
  State of the Union address,
    79-80
  veto power, 8, 79, 86, 149,
    150
  see also Executive branch;
    Senate president; *and*
    specific presidents
Press secretary, 70, 74
Proxy voting, 61
Public Law, 149

Q

Quorum
  definition, 149
  rules, 60-61

R

Rayburn House Office Building,
  110, 115
Reagan revolution, 37
Reagan, Ronald, 80, 81, 86, 94
Reaganomics, 79, 80, 86, 88
Referral, types of, 49-50
Republican Conference
  committee organization of,
    40-42
  role of, 36, 39, 41

Republicans
    Committee on Committees, 40, 42
    National Congressional Committee, 41-42
    National Senatorial Committee, 42
    party organizations on Capitol Hill, 39, 40, 41, 42
    Policy Committee, 40, 41, 42
    Senate committees, 42
Resolutions
    concurrent, 148
    continuing, 148
    definition, 149
    joint, 148
Reynolds, Mel, 54
Rodino, Peter, 60
Rolling quorum, 61
Roosevelt, Franklin D., 80, 85
Rule, definition, 149
Russell Senate Office Building, 112, 115

S

Security on Capitol Hill, 112-113
Select committees, role of, 50-51, 130
Senate
    amendment of bills in, 5
    bells and signals for floor action, 116-117
    confirmation hearings, 56-58, 64
    course of legislation through, 2-6
    debate in, 5, 35
    galleries, attendance at, 116
    informality of, 5, 35
    leadership positions in, 30-31, 33, 36-39
    majority leader, 31-32, 33, 35-36, 37-38
    majority whip, 32, 33, 39
    minority leader, 31-32, 33, 38
    minority whip, 32, 33, 39
    office buildings, 112
    party organizations, 39-41, 42-43
    personal staff in, 71-72
    president, 31, 33, 36, 149
    president pro tempore, 31, 33, 36-37, 149
Senate committees
    Aging (Select Committee), 50, 51, 123, 131
    Agriculture, Nutrition, and Forestry, 47, 123
    Appropriations, 91, 92, 94, 98-99, 123-124
    Armed Services, 94, 124
    Banking, Housing, and Urban Affairs, 124-125
    Budget, 92, 94, 99, 125
    changes in membership on, 53-56
    Commerce, Science, and Transportation, 125
    Democrat, 43
    Energy and Natural Resources, 55, 56, 125-126
    Environment and Public Works, 126
    Ethics (Select Committee), 51, 130
    Finance, 2, 38, 50, 62, 126-127
    Foreign Relations, 56, 127
    Governmental Affairs, 62, 127-128
    Indian Affairs (Select Committee), 50, 51, 128
    Intelligence (Select Committee), 50, 51, 130
    Judiciary, 56, 64, 128

Index

Labor and Human Resources, 128-129
number of, 46
Republican, 42
Rules and Administration, 37, 129
select, 50-51, 130-131
Small Business, 129
standing, 47
Veterans' Affairs, 130
see also Joint committees
Senators, constituency size, 1
Separation of powers, 79, 93, 95
Sequestration, 95-96, 150
Social security legislation, 2
Spence, Floyd, 55
Speaker of the House, 31-34
Staff on Capitol Hill
administrative, 71-72, 74
budgets for, 71, 72, 74
committee, 73, 74
contact with elected officials through, 65, 68
director, 74
experience of, 73
general counsel, 74
growth of, 65
influence and power of, 69-70, 74
press secretary, 67, 74
professional, 74
profile of, 66, 68
reduction of, 65, 73
salaries of, 71
rights and privileges of, 66, 68
of support agencies (information staff), 67, 69, 75-77
types of, 67-70
see also Personal staff
Standing committees
appropriations, 47-49, 63, 91, 92, 98-100
authorizations, 47-48, 63, 91, 98-100
changes in, 46
oversight responsibilities, 62-63
and President's influence in legislative process, 89-90
subcommittees, 47, 49
views and estimates, 99
State of the Union address, 80
Stennis, John, 94
Stock market crash of 1987, 100
Study committees
joint, 48
select, 48
Sunbelt Caucus, 44
Superfund, 63
Supreme Court, role in legislative process, 8, 103

T

Term limits
House committee chairpersons, 42, 43, 53
House subcommittee chairpersons, 43, 53
Speaker of the House, 32
Thomas, Clarence, 56
Thurmond, Strom, 37
Timmons, William, 85
Tower, John, 64
Transportation
to Capitol Hill, 109-110
deregulation, 86
Metro subway system, 109-110
Treasury, Department of, 90

U

U.S. Capitol building, access for physically disabled, 113-114

V

Veto, presidential, 8, 79, 85, 86, 149, 150
Vice president, as president of the Senate, 36
Vietnam conflict, 56, 91
Views and estimates, 98, 150
Visitors, access on Capitol Hill, 113
Vote
   recorded, 149
   teller, 150

W

Washington, George, 79
Watergate, 56, 91
Webster, Daniel, 103

Wexler, Anne, 88
Whip notice, 36
White House
   Office of Congressional Relations, 81, 83, 86
   Office of Legislative Affairs, 84, 87
   Office of Public Liaison, 88
Whitewater hearings, 63
Wilson, Woodrow, 45, 79
Windfall profits tax, 86
Women and women's issues, 55-56
Wright, Jim, 34

Z

Zone whips, 36

NOTES

The New Dynamics of Congress

To order copies of this book, complete the order form on the reverse of this coupon, using the charts at right to figure the cost of your order.

Please make your check or money order payable to The Woods Institute, and mail it with this coupon to the address on the order form.

Please allow 4–6 weeks for delivery, or call to make special arrangements.

Quantity	
1–9	$17.95 ea.
10–99	$15.95 ea.
100+	$13.95 ea.

Shipping & Handling	
1–9	$4.00
10–25	$6.00
26–99	$8.00

The New Dynamics of Congress

To order copies of this book, complete the order form on the reverse of this coupon, using the charts at right to figure the cost of your order.

Please make your check or money order payable to The Woods Institute, and mail it with this coupon to the address on the order form.

Please allow 4–6 weeks for delivery, or call to make special arrangements.

Quantity	
1–9	$17.95 ea.
10–99	$15.95 ea.
100+	$13.95 ea.

Shipping & Handling	
1–9	$4.00
10–25	$6.00
26–99	$8.00

The New Dynamics of Congress

To order copies of this book, complete the order form on the reverse of this coupon, using the charts at right to figure the cost of your order.

Please make your check or money order payable to The Woods Institute, and mail it with this coupon to the address on the order form.

Please allow 4–6 weeks for delivery, or call to make special arrangements.

Quantity	
1–9	$17.95 ea.
10–99	$15.95 ea.
100+	$13.95 ea.

Shipping & Handling	
1–9	$4.00
10–25	$6.00
26–99	$8.00

ORDER FORM

Name _____

Organization _____

Address _____

City _____ State _____ Zip _____

Country _____

FAX _____

Telephone _____

The Woods Institute
2231 California Street NW
Washington, DC 20008
FAX 202/483-0424
202/483-6167

Quantity _____

Unit Price _____

Total _____

S & H _____

Total Enclosed _____

ORDER FORM

Name _____

Organization _____

Address _____

City _____ State _____ Zip _____

Country _____

FAX _____

Telephone _____

The Woods Institute
2231 California Street NW
Washington, DC 20008
FAX 202/483-0424
202/483-6167

Quantity _____

Unit Price _____

Total _____

S & H _____

Total Enclosed _____

ORDER FORM

Name _____

Organization _____

Address _____

City _____ State _____ Zip _____

Country _____

FAX _____

Telephone _____

The Woods Institute
2231 California Street NW
Washington, DC 20008
FAX 202/483-0424
202/483-6167

Quantity _____

Unit Price _____

Total _____

S & H _____

Total Enclosed _____